A Boat for
BENNY
BY MARY COTTER

For Fíona,

With all good wishes.

Mary Cotter 03/11/24.

This book is dedicated to the memory of
my friend Paul Mulcahy [1951-2023].

'Let it be.'

The author wishes to acknowledge the support of Wexford Co. Council, the Irish Writers' Centre and the Arts Council.

Mary Cotter © 2024

CONTENTS

Chapter 1	1
Chapter 2	9
Chapter 3	19
Chapter 4	34
Chapter 5	56
Chapter 6	61
Chapter 7	78
Chapter 8	86
Chapter 9	98
Chapter 10	113
Chapter 11	117
Chapter 12	122
Chapter 13	132
Chapter 14	137
Chapter 15	146
Chapter 16	154
Chapter 17	164
Chapter 18	168
Chapter 19	172
Chapter 20	177
Chapter 21	179
Chapter 22	183
Chapter 23	189
Chapter 24	195
Chapter 25	198
Chapter 26	208

A Boat for Benny

One

I never wanted to be born. The womb was a five-star hotel. I had a place to rest, swim, sleep and be fed. I had company, too – because my twin was with me, I was never lonely. Sometimes, she went to sleep while I was swimming. That was fine because I always knew she would wake up. She was always there. She was my true north. Nothing could ever happen to me while my sister was close.

One day, alarm bells went off for both of us. Of course, she left the womb first. I was scared and hung back. I wanted to stay in the perfect home, but I had no choice. I arrived into a blinding world, hardly able to breathe. They whipped me away to the special baby unit. It was full of machines and tiny scraps of humanity like me.

My sister was nowhere near. I screamed inside myself, but they didn't hear me. The nurses had to listen to the monitors and the alarms, as I went through one crisis after another. Their hands were kind. How gently they rubbed my bony arms and warmed my feet. They watched my chest rise and fall. Their faces were grim as they took off my oxygen mask. Then they relaxed, and Mam came to see me.

She came in a wheelchair pushed by Dad. Mam was holding my sister. She held the baby up to the side of my glass cot so I could see her. She was fast asleep. I breathed deep and strong. I wanted them to see that I was a fine boy. Dad put his big hand into my cot. He rubbed my head and caught my hand. I held on very tight. I wanted him to know that I was happy to see them all.

Mam held me in one arm while my sister was in the other. We were wrapped up like onions, but I still felt the safety I'd experienced in our first home.

When I weighed five pounds, we were allowed to go home. Our new home was huge. There were so many rooms for different activities. The magic of the womb was its being designed to cope with many activities in a small space!

Some people face Mecca to pray. My sister was my Mecca. I looked for her all the time. I wanted to see her when we were being fed. We had fun in the bath and having our nappies changed. She wanted to be on her own sometimes, just like before. But I never wanted to be on my own. My eyes followed her. She was happy on her own, but I wanted her near me. I felt brave and strong when I could see her.

When we could roll around the floor, I moved towards her. Crawling was faster than rolling. She was able to crawl before I was. She pulled herself around the floor and picked up stuff to put in her mouth. Sometimes, she crawled back and hit me with a teething ring. She didn't mean any harm. She was just better at exploring than I was. I crawled. I walked. She was always a step ahead of me. Mam worried a bit about me, always following Ellen.

'Justin, he follows her all the time.'

'He wants to be near her because he learns from her.'

'Doesn't he have his own ideas?'

'He had a tough start. Remember how tiny he was? He's just catching up.'

Mam said no more. She was thinking – and already knew – you couldn't be someone else's shadow. I would have to learn that the world was mine to explore in my own way. Still, I was happy to follow Ellen all the time. Sometimes, she watched TV on her own. I didn't like the talking buses and the noise, but Ellen did. I liked Peppa Pig and her family. Her brother was much smaller than Peppa, but I was the same size as Ellen, and we were the same age. She wouldn't watch Peppa because it was too babyish, she said.

Santa brought Duplo. I loved the bricks that were big enough for clumsy fingers. They fit together. I could make a car and a trailer. But Ellen didn't want to play Duplo. I couldn't believe it. I showed her all the magic things I could build with it – if she just watched me, she would get the idea. But Ellen preferred her ideas, and wanted wooden bricks to build towers. It didn't matter that I could build great towers with Duplo. She got the wooden bricks and enjoyed them as much as I did the Duplo. When we were both sitting on the floor, building with our preferred materials, we were calm and happy. We played close to each other, but not together. I learned to tell her how good she was at building, and she said the same to me.

One day, she threw a brick at me because I was singing, and I had to have stitches. Mam was cross, and Ellen was sorry.

I played Duplo on my own or with Mam. Dad built towers with Ellen. Slowly, it began to dawn on me that Ellen and I were two different people. Though we had started together in the most beautiful place in the world, we had to move on. When we learned to talk, I asked her about it.

'I'm busy being me. I am Ellen.'

'I have a special place for you in my heart.'

'I know that. But you like Duplo, and I like wooden bricks. You like some different things, because we are different people.'

This was hard for me to hear. We had started as two separate dots growing together in a small space. We loved each other in Mam's tummy. Now, the memories of the wonderful nine months spent in the five-star hotel grew smaller and smaller in my memory. They were still there, but Ellen had spun them into a small, distant planet. Ellen was a loner. She would charge through life, and I would have to find my own way. She came out into the world first and stayed beside Mam in the hospital while I was far away, getting special care. She didn't snuffle for long, even if she fell and banged her head. She got on with her next mission. Ellen was a leader, and I was a follower. She trusted the world because it made sense to her. I would have to find my own way, because I couldn't always watch Ellen. Sometimes, she fell and cut her knee, climbed up on the presses, and fell many times. She didn't care. She was always trying something new. I waited for Ellen to try something before I took a chance myself. She often failed because she took on tasks too difficult for our age.

But failing didn't stop her. She just tried again

A Boat for Benny

another day.

I liked to sit on the floor and build with my Duplo. I wanted to feel safe and protected all the time. I needed to be able to see and hear Mam or Dad. I liked to keep the buildings for a few days. I added to them all the time. I built streets and roads and watched the figures stay where I had placed them. Dad liked to sit on the floor with me. I told stories about what was happening to the trucks, cars and people. I talked to myself and made the figures talk to me.

Ellen, meanwhile, had courage. I wanted to have a bit of her power to try new things.

I felt comfortable when I checked my Duplo town every morning. I liked what I recognised. A smile came into my head when I realised I had built my town from nothing, just my ideas. One day, I asked myself what would happen if I broke up my Lego town and started again with a new idea. I could try to build an airport. Airports are always busy. Planes are arriving and leaving all the time. It would be exciting to have so much happening and changing.

But, the houses with the gardens had taken a long time. The sheds were complicated because of the roofs. My wild idea to break it up faded from my head. I stuck with what I knew. I could only make minor changes and additions.

I talked to Mam.

'I wish I was brave like Ellen.'

'Ellen is herself. You are your own self.'

'I want to be brave and strong like she is.'

'Everyone is different. We all have special talents.'

'You're good at knitting.'

'And Dad is very good at fixing engines.'

'Mam, I have no dare in me. I'm always afraid of trying new things in case they go wrong.'

'Benny, you're a small boy. I see how good you are at Duplo. I notice how you keep your toys tidy.'

'Yes, but people notice Ellen. She has a strong voice. She is so busy doing what she wants, she never feels afraid.'

'Everyone feels afraid, Benny. I couldn't fix an engine, and Dad couldn't knit a cardigan or a baby's blanket.'

'I'll talk to Dad tonight. He might have another idea to help me.'

'Just be you and enjoy yourself.'

Going to the swimming pool was a great treat. My parents held us tightly, but we could still feel the wetness and the splash. I wanted to remember the five-star hotel, and I did, but I couldn't go back to the womb. I would have to stay where I was.

There was some good news, though – Ellen was afraid of the water. She howled and shivered, kicked the water, and kicked my dad. Mam put her hand under my back, and I leaned on her. I could see Mam's face and the blue roof of the pool. I kicked my feet.

Ellen cried until she was dried and dressed. I was wrapped in a huge towel. I wanted to return to the water, but it was time to go. I couldn't wait to go back again. Until we did, I pretended that the bath at home was a pool, and stretched out in it.

The water was a challenge for Ellen. I had not been afraid in the pool because Mam was holding me. The next time we went, Ellen asked for Mam to help her. Dad worked with me.

'Lie back in the water, Benny. You can't sink because I have my hand under your back.'

A Boat for Benny

I stretched and looked at the ceiling.

'You're good in the water, Benny. Lie still. I'll take my hand away for just one second, and you will stay afloat.'

The noise in my head was telling me to grab onto him. I didn't know how Ellen got on, but that didn't matter. I looked up into Dad's eyes. I trusted him to keep me safe.

'There's my brave boy,' Dad said. 'You trusted the water.'

'No, Dad, I trusted you.'

I didn't know if Ellen lay back on her own. For once, I was doing something on my own. I began to realise that there was no competition between Ellen and me. I had to become my own best self.

Ellen got used to the water, and we joined a swimming class. I was the first to put my head in the water, but Ellen was the first to swim alone. In the future, I might be quicker at other things.

I would listen for a little voice in my head which might whisper, 'Do it your way, Benny. Your way is best for you.'

At playschool, we made friends. Ellen's friend, Cassie, had long hair and wore glasses. She came on a playdate. We could all play together, Mam said. Cassie didn't like Duplo or Lego. The girls played with dolls and dressed them. I was not very fond of dolls, but I wanted to play with Cassie. I made cots for the dolls and even dining room furniture. I tried to stay near the girls, but they smiled and went off to eat jam sandwiches in the kitchen.

I should find someone to bring home to play with me. I didn't like people with runny noses or coughs. I knew that I couldn't get an exact match for me. Even my twin wasn't an exact match. I picked a boy called Howard. He did a lot of talking, but I liked to be quiet. I figured that he could talk to Mam if I ran out of things to say. He was full of ideas about planets, stars and the universe.

Howard arrived with a remote-control car. Oh, joy. I fetched mine, and we raced them up and down the hall. Ellen cried. Mam said I should let her play with my car for a few minutes. Those few minutes seemed very long. In the end, Ellen crashed into Howard's car. He didn't mind, he said. He was bored with the cars. We all went to watch Thomas the Tank Engine.

I'm like Thomas – a small engine who is quite happy. Ellen is like James – the big, powerful engine who is more confident. Howard is stuck in the repair shop and still needs a name. I can name him when I know what kind of engine he is. He might not be a train at all. He might be in charge of everything, like the Fat Controller. No, I don't like that idea. The Fat Controller is bossy, and I don't like bossy people.

It will all work out. Sometimes, I have to wait for an idea or a plan. Now, I'm good at two things: swimming and Howard.

Two

We were five years old, and it was time to go to school. Mam brought us to Dunnes to get our uniforms. We were kitted out quickly. When we got home, Mam made us wear the whole uniform and stand beside each other while she and Dad took pictures on their phones. They wanted us to have rucksacks on our backs and lunch boxes in our hands. The shirt collars were stiff and rubbed against our necks. I opened the top button, but Mam said that wouldn't do. The tie wasn't so bad. It was on a piece of elastic, so you could pull it like a clown's nose for fun. Ellen and I popped them up and down and laughed loudly. Mam was not pleased.

We had to get black shoes that would last the winter. I got ones with laces and plenty of room at the top. Ellen got strapped ones, but they were not pretty. My trousers covered the grey socks, but Ellen's grey tights were dull.

'Mam, they're awful,' she cried.

'They must be grey, though I don't know why,' Mam said. 'Grey is an awful colour on children.'

'Benny is lucky, his trousers cover the grey.'

'God give me strength,' Mam said. 'You'll never have to wear anything grey ever again. It's just for school.'

Mam said we needed small, neat rucksacks. I wanted a big one because I was a trainee astronaut, and Ellen wanted a big one because she was bringing Gogo, her toy monkey, to school with her. She wouldn't listen when Mam said there would be plenty of toys in the school.

We were excited about going. Lots of people from our playgroup would be there. The place would not be like a foreign country. We would recognise people – until we found out the devastating truth. The truth will not set you free. It will give you a stomach ache!

Mam left it 'til the last minute. She waited until Dad was home from the garage and had washed his face. They talked about school. We were buzzing.

'School is for big children,' said Mam.

'We know. We're five now.'

'A girl is big enough to attend a girls' school.'

'And you, Benny, are big enough to attend a boys' school.'

'That's wrong,' Ellen said. 'Boys and girls go to the same school. Don't be silly, Mam.'

'In some towns that happens, but here in Derrybawn, the boys go to St Declan's and the girls go to Mount Joseph.'

'Pick a school we can go to together,' I said.

'There isn't one anywhere near here.'

Ellen and I were upset.

'Mam, it doesn't make any sense. Boys and girls together is how it should be,' Ellen said.

'We're used to boys and girls together from playschool. We have mixed friends,' I said. 'I want to be with Ellen.'

'I want to be with Benny.'

'Justin, do we have two babies here? I thought we had big five-year-olds.'

'You'll only be in school until one-thirty, then you'll have all the afternoon and evening to be together,' said Dad.

'In fairness,' Mam said, 'sometimes you like to play with other people, and sometimes you two fight.'

We knew that was correct. But no one was listening to us. They didn't notice the sadness in our voices. We thought we would be in the same class and school.

'Benny and I are twins. We are special friends,' Ellen said sadly.

'I'm not just her brother. I'm her twin,' I emphasised.

'You waited until the last minute to tell us. I'm definitely bringing Gogo with me now. If there is no Benny, there will be Gogo.'

We didn't know that Mam bawled her eyes out that night. Dad had to make tea for her at bedtime. We eventually fell asleep, since we'd been walking in the woods that day for hours. I think they planned it. We were so exhausted, we were too tired to cry or kick up a fuss.

School was too big and too bright. Our schools were beside each other. Dad walked in with Ellen, and Mam walked in with me. I could see the big bulge in Ellen's rucksack. She had Gogo with her, but I had Mam. Mam was worth a lot of Gogos.

Miss Atkins, my teacher, didn't like fuss. She had a long, green dress that swished when she walked. She took me by the hand and sat me down at a table with two boys. Mam was hanging around, but Miss

Atkins knew those outside the classroom were the best parents. I saw the Lego on the table before me, and the boys building a boat. I joined in. If there was Lego, it was a safe place for me.

It's true that I fell in love with Miss Atkins. It happened instantly, and the feeling overwhelmed me. From the first day, I liked her green dress that whispered as she walked. She had big, grey eyes that were always calm. She had long, red hair. Some days, she wore it up in a bun and other times, it hung around her shoulders. She made us feel safe. We all wanted to please her. Most of the time, she behaved like a second mother. Her voice was compelling. Even if she was only whispering, we strained to catch every word. She would only use that voice when telling a story, since it wouldn't be so good for learning sounds or singing.

Sometimes, she changed. If a boy threw things, hit another boy or said bad words, she was beside him in a flash. She didn't shout, just looked. Her face was so sad and hurt that we were all sorry, even if we weren't the guilty ones.

In her whispery voice, she sniffed and said, 'I'm so disappointed.'

She walked back to her table, and the culprits were shamed.

Wasn't it very clever? Without raising her voice, she got her message across. We were so sorry for hurting her feelings that we were stunned into obedience.

Ellen's teacher was Miss Carmody. Ellen loved her because she thought Ellen was a great girl. She was good at sorting boxes, making shapes and colouring in. Ellen often came home with stickers for good behaviour, reading and speaking out loud. I wasn't surprised, because she was so good at everything.

I got stickers as well, for tidying up and being helpful. Mam and Dad were delighted that we were both getting on well. Ellen and I were proud of ourselves and each other. I could see how Miss Carmody suited Ellen because she always came home with a smile on her face. She said she could tell Miss Atkins suited me because I was relaxed going to and coming from school.

We settled into school life, making new friends.

I was with Miss Atkins for two years and Miss Geary for two more, and then I had a male teacher.

Mr O'Toole was a hero.

I cannot say I loved Mr O'Toole, but he was my kind of man. He loved PE and Art, and he read stories aloud for us. He made me believe in the magic of reading. There was complete silence when he read The Hobbit, as we listened to Bilbo's adventures.

I believe a teacher is an actor – the classroom is their stage, and the children make up the audience. Nobody wants to see the same performance every day. Of course, the subjects can't change and must be developed, but a little imagination can go a long way.

While Irish, English and Maths had to be built on step by step, other subjects could be sandwiched in between them. Irish Reading was difficult as the sounds were not the same as in English. After a hard slog with a new piece, Mr O'Toole might read a story for us. We liked stories from Irish mythology. We didn't realise that he was teaching the History programme at the same time – it was pure bliss for us.

We could look forward to singing, drawing and

reading on our own, plus painting and football as treats to relieve the difficult work. Mr O'Toole was fair, and we trusted him. He understood that Howard's mother had an unusual career and that his dad took his university work very seriously. Howard might have worn the same shirt for a full week, and his fingers may have been grubby, but that wasn't his fault. He knew that Matt's father worked away a lot and that Matt missed him terribly. He understood that being a twin wasn't always easy for me.

I had two good friends. Howard had grown on me over the years, and while he still talked a lot, I had plenty to say now. Matt Evans lived close to me. These two grew on me the way a plant grows on fertile ground. Matt played chess and, though it took a long time, I eventually learned strategies. I understood that you had to plan your moves in chess; you had to watch out for the consequences of your actions.

I still don't know how Howard and I became friends. I remembered the day he brought his remote-control car to my house. He believed he was a genius. He liked black holes, dinosaurs and computers. He was awkward. He couldn't kick a ball to save his life. But Howard had a great strategy – he simply didn't care, even if he tripped over his feet and people laughed at him. He didn't boast or swagger, even when the class mocked him for always getting ten out of ten on his tests.

I wished I was not so concerned about what people thought of me. Wanting to be liked occupied my thoughts a lot. I thought there might be a book I could read, but everything in the library was all about adventures. There were books on habitats and cats of all sizes, but I was not a cat!

I watched other boys in school and from this, I discovered that people were not the same. Every boy was different. Some, like Howard, were very bright, and everything came easy to them. Other chaps struggled to learn to read and do Maths. Some lads could do joined-up writing when they were eight, and others' work could only be read by the teacher.

When Ellen brought her friends home, the same was true for them. Thinking didn't help. Howard and Matt spent no time worrying about themselves. I wanted to be invisible, to roam the earth as a spirit so that my good or bad actions flew under the radar so much that I was overlooked.

My parents loved me, and my twin sister blew hot and cold. I had Matt for the strategy and Howard for the coolness. All in all, my life was fine – if I could accept that.

We headed into Fifth Class to a new teacher, Mr O'Gara. He talked Irish all day long. By this stage, we had six years of Irish under our belts. When we were little, it was good fun. It was all songs, games and little rhymes. Our parents loved it when we arrived home, knowing new names for our colours. We even had a rhyme that our parents had learned themselves.

However, all that changed when we had to learn to read in Irish. We could read English well, since we spoke it all the time and our books were in English. We sang, played football and ate our meals in it. When we started to read, we learned all the sounds of English. We knew the sound of the word 'she'.

Life became very complicated when we discovered that in Irish, 'si' – meaning 'she' – sounded the same as the English 'she', while 'beidh' – the Irish word for 'will be' – sounded the same as 'beg'.

All the fun, games and rhymes disappeared. Irish became a trial. I loved words, stories and writing, but doing these in a second language puts pressure on everyone. Mr O'Gara taught everything in Irish. We had to stand up, sit down, open our exercise books and do arithmetic in Irish. If we were slow to learn the irregular verbs, he took time off Maths to make us keep at it. I was not too pleased that he cut the Art classes by thirty minutes to do more Irish. A sense of grievance pervaded the classroom.

When he cut out one PE class completely, some parents objected, and he was forced to reinstate the second one. He was livid, and retaliated by stopping all painting. He turned us off Irish for life.

Mr O'Toole, on the other hand, employed a method much more suitable for young boys. He believed in sandwiches. He followed something difficult with something pleasant. The day began with mental arithmetic, and then Irish followed – but it mainly was conversation. We spent plenty of time on Maths. We sang a few songs after the first break. The English time was varied and exciting. He would then do DEAR – drop everything and read – and we would do so in silence for twenty minutes. Mr O'Toole got all the work done, and still kept the children happy.

Matt noticed the consequences of his actions very often in Mr O'Gara's class. He delayed us going out for football if we didn't understand the Irish grammar. Even ungainly fellows like Howard wanted to get out into the fresh air. He stayed with us into Sixth Class, where now it was all about Confirmation: the gifts of the Spirit, the tongues of fire, the oil of chrism and the bishop. I missed Mr O'Toole. I imagined how much of the Lord of the Rings he would have gotten through by Christmas. Here I was, longing for the Lord but overwhelmed by the Spirit. Howard thought that was a clever play on words.

I thought of the end of the year, and the prospect of heading into secondary school. That would be an eye-opener, because in the secondary school, boys and girls would be together. After eight years in single-sex schools, the powers that be decreed that when our hormones were raging most ferociously, that was the best time to bring us together. My parents were delighted. They believed it was more natural. They were not delighted, however, about the cost of the uniform. There was no hopping into Dunnes this time for generic pinafores and pants.

But wait, I'm getting ahead of myself. We still had to take an Entrance Exam, and Mr O'Gara wasn't too worried about the results.

'The top sixty pupils will be mixed into two classes. In First Year, you will take all subjects. At the end of First Year, the classes will then be sorted grade-wise. The pupils with the highest results will be in 2A. The next lot of thirty will be in 2B.'

Howard wanted to know what the difference was.

'B does the same work as A, but takes things a little slower. That's all.'

Well, guys who had never done a tap of work were suddenly doing their homework. There was no mention of C or D, while E and F might not have existed. A few of my class decided that they would slack off and be cool – but their attitude soon changed when they heard they could be expelled from secondary school.

We did the entrance exams in March, and were 'good and perfect Christians' by the end of April. All that remained was for us to graduate.

A Boat for Benny

Three

I was all set. I would wear my decent chinos and a navy shirt to the Graduation Mass. All the girls from Sixth Class would be there as well.

Matt and I were strolling home that day without a care in the world. Our eight years of primary school dipped under the horizon like a well-behaved summer sun.

'I have a bit of news,' Matt said.

The tone of his voice made me suspicious.

'I won't be going to the Academy.'

It fell like a stone, and walloped me in the chest.

'My dad has got a new job in Galway. I'll be going to school there.'

'I was sure we'd be going on together, Matt.'

'Won't you have Howard and your sister? There'll be new lads in from country schools. You'll be made up.'

'I won't be made up. We've been together a long time, Matt. You taught me chess. You have the strategies. Holy God!'

We walked on in silence.

I had nothing to say because I was already sad. Matt was dependable. He didn't have many different moods. He did have a Monday face, so I knew to keep quiet then. The rest of the week, though, he was easy to talk to. When we went to his house, he heated up macaroni cheese, we drank milk and then set up our chess game.

But I wasn't going to be winsome and emotional. I didn't cry or beg him to stay. When I got home, I told Mam, who just hugged me. It's good to have a mother who knows the limitations of speech. In bed that night, I was tormented thinking of what other changes the universe had in store for me: new school, new uniform, new girls, new lads, and no chess partner.

The Mass was in the big church. We sang, 'The higher you build your barriers / The taller I become'. There was no pupil of the year business. We all got a medal for finishing the year. Then we headed into the Community Centre. The noise was deafening. Parents milled about around the long tables, picking up cups of tea and small cakes. The parents were all dressed up. Mam had got her hair done that afternoon, and Dad was wearing his best blue shirt. Though Mam was talking to her friends, she was able to keep an eye on us. There would be war if we let her down in public, so we were on our best behaviour.

There were big bottles of Coke, Haribo sweets and cheese and onion crisps. Howard, Matt and I stocked up. The area around the stage was crowded with graduates. We were on the road to a sugar high, and got a bit giddy from all the sugary Haribo. Once you start eating them, you can't stop. Though the Coke was Zero, it still had power. Matt, Howard and I had a burping competition. Mam looked in my direction, so I went to the bathroom.

As the evening went on, some of the girls got emotional. They were weeping and saying, 'Oh, Mrs O'Connell, I'll miss you so much' and 'Mrs O'Connell, I don't want to attend the Irish school. My parents are making me go.'

We were not hanging on to Mr O'Gara, and instead were wondering which class would have him in September. Those boys already had our sympathy. They didn't have a clue what lay ahead of them.

Ellen and Cassie were busy spotting talent. A fellow called Schooner Thomas had arrived in our class after Christmas. He was from South Carolina and was very tall. It seemed that he was 'the dude'. I blushed to see my twin watch him as he moved around the room, but it was her business. Mam saw her, though. She and Cassie followed Schooner, but pretended they were looking for another girl.

Mam gave her what for when we got home.

'I saw you. The eyes in your head were out on sticks watching that American. Giggling and smiling, you and Cassie. Not a bit of discretion.'

Ellen blushed, and her eyes were red. But she didn't cry. Ellen had iron in her backbone. Mam had not spotted that my eyes followed Cassie everywhere. She was wearing her Confirmation dress – it was blue denim and fitted her perfectly.

Ellen told me she would not let Mam see her ogling anyone again. She was cross with herself for being so obvious. She whispered to me that she was crazy about Schooner. I didn't tell her that I was madly in love with Cassie, that her presence in our house drove me demented with love and longing. In September, I could watch her without our mother present.

Ellen was embarrassed, and that rarely happened. She was usually well-informed about Mam. She would use this lesson to become more circumspect in all she did.

July rolled on. Matt invited me over to camp in the garden. We played chess in the tent 'til our eyes were sore. Then, we lay in our sleeping bags on the grass and watched the stars.

'Is your new school co-ed, Matt?'

'No, all boys. My dad went there.'

'Do they have a good chess club?

'Benny, there's no chess club. It's a mad rugby school.'

'You're not a rugby guy, Matt.'

'Too true. I'm a chess and microscope person, Benny. Dad knows that already. I've no interest in team sports. I do like cross-country running. On the plus side, I have cousins there. They'll help me settle in.'

Soon, the removal vans arrived, and in a flurry of days, Matt was no more.

I had walked to school with him for years. We had enjoyed Mr O'Toole's class together, and suffered under Mr O'Gara's rule. Matt had been easy to get on with and tolerated me.

Still, there was always Howard, and he was available. I thought that would be fine for August, and that I could make a new friend in September. I was used to Howard. I was not too fond of surprises, and Howard was constant. I could depend on him since we were little. I might even make a new girlfriend as well.

Ellen was out nearly all the time. She was in Cassie's house, or Cassie was in our house. There were other girls with them, too. They never spoke to me, acted as if I was invisible. That would have suited me in the past, but I was a growing boy now. I wanted girls to look at me the way they looked at Schooner. I even grew my fringe long so it hung over one eye, but it wasn't cool.

It wasn't so much other girls as Cassie. I wanted to talk to her. I wanted Ellen to evaporate and leave Cassie here with me. I wanted to show her my good side. I could be a great version of myself if I could talk out of earshot of my twin. But Ellen and Cassie had been glued to each other since they were three. They shared nail varnish, clothes, magazines, beds and PJs! There was an intimacy about girls' friendships that left me scared and wary. The beds and the PJs were the ultimate horrors.

September loomed. You couldn't go to Dunnes for the secondary uniform, and had to shop in Gerraghy's Outfitters. Mam had been saving for months. We started with the blazers, saying she wanted to face that issue first. One hundred euro each!

'How much without the crest?'

'You can't get one without the crest,' Lonie Dawson said.

'How much for just a crest?'

'They're not available.'

Ellen's skirt would be seventy, my trousers fifty, and PE gear ninety each.

Mam's face was getting very red. We knew the signs of frustration.

'Come here to me, Lila,' said Lonie. 'I know a few parents who are selling second-hand uniforms. Take those phone numbers. No insult intended, but the new ones are daylight robbery.'

Insulted! Not a bit of it. Mam was grateful to her old school friend. I had been worried that she would explode when she heard the prices. I was watching her face. Ellen noticed nothing because she was on her phone all the time.

Mam enjoyed herself. She got two blazers, a skirt, my PE gear, two jumpers and school ties. She bought my trousers from Lonie, but walked home with a smile.

Ellen wasn't pleased.

'Mam, I'm going to be a laughing stock. All my friends will have new uniforms, and I'll be wearing someone else's castoffs.'

'Well, madam, if you want new ones, you buy them yourself.'

That stopped Ellen, though I could see her point. The new skirts we had seen in the shop had sharp pleats, but Ellen's skirt was flat. Everyone would know it wasn't new. Both jumpers were okay, not worn-looking at all. I reckoned that appearance was more important to girls. They talked about lipstick, eyeliner and nail varnish. Girls who were good at Maths, English, Geography and Science still worried about how they looked in front of their friends.

Mam felt sorry for Ellen, with the non-existent pleats in her skirt. We arrived home one evening to a kitchen full of steam (I was not familiar with the workings of a steam iron). Hanging on the kitchen door was a skirt that looked nothing like it had before.

'Mam, what's happened?'

'Now, Ellen, I steamed the pleats back in. A steam iron is a gift from the Great Mother in the sky.'

Ellen ran upstairs, and soon we could hear delighted squeals. She paraded into the kitchen, showing off her sharp pleats and neat skirt.

'Mother, you're a genius.'

'Now, Ellen. The pleats won't last, but this is what we'll do. I'll use the steam iron on Sundays, and you will have week-long pleats.'

At this point, tears rolled down Ellen's face. My twin, who never cried!

'You'll get the year out of it, anyway. Once you grow out of it, I'll buy you a new one. You put up with the grey tights for eight years, Ellen. Bad pleats would have been a double whammy.'

We sat down and had tea and a slice of coffee cake. Peace reigned.

In fairness, I was pleased that I got new trousers, but it made no difference. I wouldn't look at other lads' trousers, and they wouldn't bother about where my blazer came from.

More black shoes were required, but at least Ellen could wear black tights now. As this was considered a fashion statement, she smiled, and all was well.

The books were the next issue. Parents were selling those on as well. Mam didn't care if there were scribbles on the cover, drawings of body parts in the margins, or if the corners were curly. She tackled those books with gusto and soon had them looking quite acceptable.

Mam cried when she saw us in our uniforms on

our first day. We were so grown-up, she said.

I have the photograph. Black matching blazers, white shirts, grey trousers for me, and a grey, black and cream skirt for Ellen. We looked as if we were going to a funeral.

I walked up myself, since Howard lived on the other side of town. Girls surrounded Ellen, and were talking non-stop and giggling. I missed Matt because we would chat quietly on the way to school – except for Mondays, when he wore his Monday face.

I headed in and sat in the hall beside Howard. We would find which group we were going to be allocated to. That would decide a lot – no As or Bs for First Years. We were divided into colour groups, and soon figured out that Blue and Gold were the top sixty. It was easy.

As the names were called, my fear increased. Howard, Ellen and several lads from my class were called for Blue. Schooner and Cassie were called for gold. Then, my name joined theirs. Someone made a mistake, and Matt was called for Gold. I thought he was back, hoped more than anything that he was, but it was just a clerical error.

By 11:30, we were ensconced in our base classrooms. Cassie sat beside me, and strangers surrounded us. I thought she would have plopped herself beside Schooner. Our tutor was Mr Flavin. In a matter of minutes, a stack of papers covered our tables. We had to accept the school rules, signing them to confirm. We all knew what the uniform was. Weren't we wearing it, for God's sake? Apparently, you could only wear your tracksuit on your PE days. Mr Flavin assured us that he knew every move his tutorial class could make every hour of every day, and we were not to assume we could blindside him.

Anyone who hadn't yet got their winter jacket was warned that the knock-off version that could be bought in Penneys for twenty euro was unacceptable. It had to be black. Navy wouldn't do, even if your mother came in and cried.

'I've seen all the tricks and delays,' he said. 'Do remind your parents that second-hand jackets will be available in the school by Halloween. Reduce, reuse and recycle.'

He handed out our timetable. We had double Irish on Monday morning, and double English on Friday afternoon. I suggested they might be changed around. I loved English, and I was already mentally starting my weekend by Friday afternoon.

He eyeballed me.

'If I were you, Cullen, I'd keep my thoughts to myself.'

I could feel Matt whispering in my ear, 'Consequences of actions – shut up, keep custody of the eyes and agree with everything.'

We were allowed to leave at lunchtime. Cassie and I walked out together, but she was not happy.

'I don't like it one bit, Benny. All those rules!'

'I shouldn't have said anything,' I replied. 'Opening my mouth was not a good idea.'

We sat on the wall, watching hundreds of kids leave.

'Come on home with me, and we can have a can of coke, Cassie.'

'I'll wait on for Ellen.'

'See you tomorrow then,' I said glumly.

'Benny, will you grab two seats by the window in the middle row for tomorrow?'

'Will do. I'll be in early.'

It wasn't much, but I took it gladly. She wanted to sit beside me. I had to warn myself that I was one of a few people she knew well, but a sense of well-being filled my chest.

Howard was waiting for me at the gate. Yes, they had the same chapter and verse, the whole shooting gallery. He knew his mother wouldn't fork out for the winter jacket. He could see trouble ahead.

But after a week, we got used to it all. Double Irish was not so bad. Miss Greyson was a great teacher, and one of the sessions was in the computer room, which suited everyone.

The Friday double English class was a tough station. Mr Finlay told us that he hated that slot. We did Julius Caesar for the first class. We read our class novel, Goodnight Mister Tom, until the bell went. It would only last 'til Christmas, he told us. Then, the Blues would take their turn. I loved the novel. When we had finished it, Mr Finlay let us watch the movie version. John Thaw was the perfect Mr Tom for me.

There was little to be seen out the windows. After a few days, Mr Finlay resorted to pulling down the blinds, reminding us they were to stay that way. At least the windows were open for the first few weeks. As we headed towards November, the staff asked us to close them. The room became stuffy. We developed a system – the girls could be off-colour at certain times, so they took turns asking to open the windows. The odd boy also had to do that to ensure they wouldn't smell a rat.

A Boat for Benny

By the end of the first week, we were exhausted. Saturday and Sunday rose like a lighthouse to save us from school and homework.

The amount of homework doled out by most teachers was daunting. We found we were too busy every evening to keep up to date. Our weekends looked threatened. A small group from Blue and Gold was asked to find out if we could be work-free for the weekend. Howard and Ellen were two of the chosen. No one could have guessed that throwing these two together would cause sparks to fly. The group came up with a homework plan and made a great job of it. It was impossible to have the whole weekend free, but if we committed to two hours on Saturday or Sunday, we would float into Monday up to date. The data came with a health warning – on no account, leave it until Sunday night. That would be lethal.

As far as I could see, Howard and Ellen had nothing in common. He had known her since we were three when he brought the remote-control car. They had been in our house for years where he was known as my friend. He was still talking about black holes, the cosmos and invertebrates. She was throwing the javelin and swimming. He arrived home with her. Mam said nothing. They drank tea and ate apples. He stopped lecturing on his favourite topics as his eyes followed Ellen everywhere. I saw them holding hands at the front gate one day. Ellen did not wear her heart on her sleeve – she kept it well hidden in the secret pocket under the waistband of her skirt.

They began to spend a lot of time together. He was in our house even when I wasn't. She continued lane-swimming on Friday nights and track and field after school. She didn't see much of Cassie. Her schedule was crammed with homework, Howard and sports. A new girl arrived into Blue. Her name was Suzanne, and she needed a buddy. She got Cassie. I wanted to go up to the office and say to Mr Hennessy that I needed a buddy, and that Cassie would be ideal – after all, I was there longer – but I didn't.

I had to face facts. Whatever fireworks had gone off when Howard and Ellen had their first conversation, it hadn't happened for Cassie. I was in a permanent state of a lit fuse, but Cassie was like a damp match.

Things took a turn for the worse when Ellen visited Howard's house. His mam had dreadlocks, two rings in her nose, and smoked a joint. His dad stayed in his office the whole time. They were allowed to go to Howard's room, which made them hot and excited. Ellen was thinking about kissing, and Howard was on the same train.

The walls were painted black. His duvet cover was adorned with gravestones. He had a skeleton hanging on a nail and the place smelled horrible. Ellen was not impressed. They lay down on his bed, and she admired the glowing stars on the ceiling. She soon forgot about the black walls. She cuddled into him and closed her eyes to block out the skeleton. They did get down to kissing, which was satisfactory for both. She was invited to stay for dinner, but a vegan plate was beyond her.

I began to meet up with Bartley, who knew Matt very well. Howard was busy with Ellen, and Cassie was seen with Suzanne morning, noon, and night. If I managed to grab a word with her in school, I had the feeling she was just being polite. We still sat beside each other, but I wanted more.

Suzanne smoked. She hitched up her skirt and flounced along the corridors. She had no time for First Year boys. If she wanted a boyfriend, she must have been looking elsewhere. Our school was known for hockey. The Junior team were all two years older than us.

A boy of thirteen looks like a boy of thirteen, even if he has had a growth spurt. He is a strange creature. His voice wobbles. He has hair growing in new places. Spots start to appear on his neck, nose and chin. His penis develops a mind of its own and makes its presence felt at the most inconvenient of times. Ellen said it was much the same for girls, apart from some details. It was the same in-between feeling. We were neither children nor adults, more like half-grown butterflies.

It would be convenient to have girls nearby when you were wondering what kind of girl attracted you. I would be happy to be near Cassie. I still liked Cassie a lot, but there would be new girls with smiles and lovely eyes. Some of them would already have chests, and that idea was exciting. Some would still be flat, but the prospect was always there. I didn't look at Cassie's chest because I would be so embarrassed if she caught me.

I thought of Cassie when I was lying in bed. Things began to happen to me. I thought emissions came from car engines, but I discovered that there were personal emissions as well. Dad was great because he put my mind at ease. It was part of growing up. He said a lot more, but it was private between father and son.

Mam talked to me as well about girls. I didn't want

to hear it, having already accepted that my penis had a mind of its own, and realising that Mam knew that.

When she was finished, I felt sorry for girls and women. They seemed to have constant reminders about their feminine aspects. That was enough information for me.

A girl of thirteen can add years to her life with eyeliner, lipstick and blusher. I began to notice that Cassie was wearing makeup. This didn't do me any good because it made her look even more beautiful in my eyes. Maybe Cassie wanted a boyfriend, too. After all, Howard was stuck to Ellen's hip.

One Wednesday afternoon, I saw Cassie walking home alone. Suzanne was watching the hockey training. I caught up with Cassie. I didn't want to whine. I wanted my words to come out in a manly fashion.

'Hi.'

'Hi, Benny.'

'I never see you these times, Cassie.'

'Ellen is with Howard all the time.'

'I'm not Ellen. I'm still around.'

'I'm friends with Suzanne now.'

'That shouldn't stop us being friends.'

'I have things on my mind. I need a girl to listen.'

I had no response to that.

'If you were a girl, I would trust you, Benny.'

I saw them, the tears standing in her eyes. I noticed the eyeliner and the grey eyeshadow, but the tears did the talking. She looked miserable.

'Come here to me,' I said, holding out my arms for a hug.

'You're the best. Do you know that, Benny?'

'Come to the cinema with me on Friday night?'

'I can't. I have plans.'

At which point she turned down her road. The moment was lost. I wouldn't get another chance to tell her how I felt until after the Junior Cert.

Later, I told Dad that I loved Cassie.

He said, 'Brutal, isn't it? Love is brutal.'

Four

Schooner didn't like me, so I stayed out of his way. I wanted nothing to do with him. The girls were still swarming around him like flies. So be it. I beat him for a place in the First Year chess team. That annoyed him. Matt had taught me so much that I had become a valuable player. I don't think Americans do subtle very well. We went for the same basket during a PE class, and he broke my wrist. I fell awkwardly, but I knew he had pushed me. His apologies were profuse, but he had done it deliberately. I played chess with my left hand. I was not giving up.

After this episode, I used some of Howard's strategies.

'All that matters is what matters to me.'

'Explain.'

'I have no interest in sport, so having two left feet doesn't matter. I'm crazy about science, but I don't talk about it. Some would call me a nerd. What do I care?'

'What about your feelings being hurt?'

'Benny, get a grip. All that matters is what matters to me. I don't let things have power over me, ever.'

I thought about what he had said. Schooner might have been the choice of the girls, but he wasn't popular with lads. He could shoot baskets using his long American arms, but I was not interested in basketball, except as a subject in the PE curriculum.

After Christmas, the activity changed to cross-country running. I liked to challenge myself. I ran for the joy of the outdoors. January was muddy, and February was cold, but I had a great time.

How soon Easter rolled around, and by the end of May, our house exams were done, and three full months of holidays stretched out before us. I helped Dad in the garage, and Ellen did some hours in the shop. Howard hung around our house. I got the feeling that he was more interested in Ellen than me. I was interested in Cassie, for all the good that did me.

By mid-August, the exam results arrived. Ellen and Cassie would be in 2A. Howard would be holding his place, and Schooner would be moving up. I would stay in 2B. The positive outcome was that Schooner was gone; the negative side was that I knew no one in my new base class.

We would not continue with every subject. We had chosen seven for our Junior Cert. Irish, English and Maths were compulsory. My choices were History, Geography, Woodwork and Art.

We walked in again on September 1st. Mr Flavin remained our tutor. We read and signed all the papers again. We had to spend ages on the timetable. Even in our class, people would be split up because of choices. All we could be sure of was that we would start every day in our base classroom.

For the first Art class, Miss Murphy had us working in pairs. We had to sketch our partners while they sketched us. I was put with a guy called Christopher. We shook hands.

'I don't know you at all,' I said. 'Are you new?'

'No. I was in Blue last year. I remember you in the primary. You're Benny, Ellen's brother.'

'How do you know my twin?'

'I've seen her in the swimming pool. She's good.'

We proceeded with the task. He was busy looking at me, but I wasn't embarrassed because I was taking in his face. The time flew by, and Miss Murphy collected our work in a large folder.

The Woodwork room was a place of beauty. The workbenches were large enough for two students. You had your vice and your own set of tools. Any electronic tools were kept under lock and key. The windows were large, and the room always felt airy. The fluorescent lights were a good idea, since we had to bend over a lot for close work and needed good light to keep the work accurate. The room smelled of oil, paint, wood shavings and stain.

We couldn't wait to start, but Mr O'Donnell cooled our heels. For the first two classes, we did nothing but listen. He explained that tools weren't toys. They were to be treated with respect.

'Just because you made a go-kart once upon a time doesn't mean you know anything about wood. By Christmas, you will be well used to my system. I'll pair you up now; the bench will be yours for the year.'

He put Christopher and me together. That was just fine. We learned the names of the tools. Hammers and saws were easy, but spokeshaves and awls were new. It was also news to me that there were two kinds of chisels: cold and wood chisels. We would not need a cold chisel, since they were only needed for concrete.

'Two options the same,' Christopher said, smiling at me.

A Boat for Benny

'Happy to be your partner,' I said.

We learned a dove-tailed joint. As soon as Mr O'Donnell was content with the accuracy, we made a polish box for home. Dove-tailed joints held the box together. We were proud to bring our constructions home to be used.

Dad was impressed with the joints. I didn't mention that Christopher's joints were beautiful compared to mine. Using the spokeshave required the vice. The wood block had to be held tightly while you held the spokes to achieve the desired curve for a fishtail. It was not a good shape for a chopping board. It was good practice, but I prefer a square or round chopping board. Once I had rubbed oil into it at home, it was ready for use. Mam found it too small and narrow. After a few weeks, it became an item at the back of a press, just taking up space.

'I like working with my hands. I work in the garage with my dad, but that's mostly cleaning and clearing,' I said.

'I like to paint and draw at home. My dad has a lathe, and I want to learn to work with wood,' Christopher replied.

I was getting to like Christopher. He was very good at painting, and his woodwork was always immaculate. While I was doing Geography, he chose Home Economics. He liked cooking. More than anything else, we both loved English. We enjoyed reading and talking about books.

'Do you remember when Mr O'Toole read The Hobbit?' I asked Christopher.

'I do. That was what got me into reading, you know.'

'The Lion, the Witch and the Wardrobe in Third

Class did it for me.'

'He was a brilliant teacher.'

'He was, and Miss Atkins was too.'

'You were an angel in the Nativity, Benny.'

'I was. How come you remember that?'

'The wings, Benny. You had huge blue wings. I drew a picture of you when I went home.'

We laughed.

'Who were you in the play?'

'I was supposed to be a star but didn't show. I spent the day vomiting at home. Such a waste of a costume. White tights, t-shirt and a silver star headdress.'

'Howard was an angel with me. Miss Atkins gave us all names.'

'You were Gabriel, the chief angel.'

'How many stars were there?'

'Maybe four. The others were all girls. I remember Ita Patterson, that's all. I was quiet when I was little. Ita was kind to me, and she sat at my table.'

I tried to think of what to say. I wanted to say something.

'Well, I think you're sound. I'm glad we have two classes together, and English as well.'

'Art is great, isn't it, and Woodwork too?'

'I don't think you're too quiet at all. It's easy to be comfortable with you.'

'Likewise,' said Christopher.

I didn't forget Howard. He came home on Fridays with me. In fairness, he had developed a keen interest in Ellen. They had a lot in common. They were both interested in science. They were top of the class in Maths, English and History. Christopher began to come round as well. And, of course, where Ellen was at the weekend, Cassie was too. Howard had let his hair grow. He had curls around his head now, and down to his shoulders. One Friday, he arrived at the house wearing jeans covered in biro drawings, a Bat Out of Hell t-shirt and a denim jacket with the sleeves cut out.

Ellen was sporting tight jeans and a top that was too small. Cassie looked very comfortable in a tracksuit. I was still in my uniform, and so was Christopher. We were lounging on couches when the folks came in. Friday night meant chips night in our house. Mam had to be introduced to Christopher, while Dad got the order sorted.

We ate everything, drank the Coke Zero and cleared up. We said we would go for a walk. In a matter of minutes, Ellen and Howard were walking along together, so Christopher, Cassie and I followed.

'Do they like each other?' I asked.

'You could say that,' Cassie giggled.

'Who do you like, Cassie?' asked Christopher.

She blushed. 'Oh, that would be telling,' she said. 'What about you guys?'

'I like boys myself,' Christopher stated.

You could have knocked me down with a feather. I hadn't a clue that he was gay! My eyes bulged out of my head while I tried to process what I had heard.

'And Christopher, what about Benny here?'

'My lips are sealed.'

Howard and Ellen were well ahead as we got to the bridge.

'I think I'll head home now, lads,' said Cassie.

Christopher and I walked back to ours.

'Does it make a difference to you?' he asked quietly.

'Why should it? You're my first gay friend. No. You're my good friend in 2B. No more to be said.'

There was much more to be said, but I didn't know what it was. This chap and I had so much in common. We liked Art, Woodwork, English and cross-country running. What was I afraid of?

I lay in bed that night with one side of my head fighting with the other. Would having a gay friend draw attention to me? I just wanted to blend in. Ellen always had been the brave one. I followed on. And then it hit me – what if he fancied me? What if it was all because he was attracted to me? I had suspected nothing. Maybe everyone in school knew. Maybe Ellen knew but hadn't told me. Did Cassie or Howard know?

Christopher phoned me the following morning.

'Come over for lunch,' he said.

I had to. Low profile or not, I needed information.

'Shattered,' he said.

'What?'

'That's how you looked last night. Benny, I don't fancy you. All is cool.'

I smiled at him then.

'You know me so well.'

'Let's be friends forever.'

'Longer than that, Chris.'

We enjoyed the spaghetti bolognese made by him from the school recipe.

'Good. There's enough left for my parents to have for their dinner.'

We went for a cycle up to the waterfall. Of course, you have to veer off the road – waterfalls like their privacy and enjoy being surrounded by nature. They have a fancy for large boulders, a significant drop and a splash pool below. The river turns towards the town, going on its merry way.

First, you listen. Half the fun is noticing the noise before you see a drop of water. Leaving the bikes, we ran over to the riverside and then we looked up. With fierce disregard, the water plunged to level ground, complaining, growling and frantic. The row continued as the water entered the splash pool. In a few moments, all was calm. The banks of the river contained it, guided it and only whispered its way along. We took pictures with our phones. We recorded the sounds, even the quiet murmur of the river.

The shots were very different when we checked them back at Christopher's house. Mine were all taken from a distance. I was always trying to cram the world into my view. Christopher's were all close-ups. He had a stone, a flower, a discarded crisp bag and graffiti, drops of water on a leaf and a pedal from his bike.

'We look at the world differently,' I said.

'Thank God,' he said. 'No clones around here.'

'Let's paint a ship at sea,' I said. 'I'd like to see how you would do that.'

'Why that theme, Benny?'

'I'm fascinated by water, and you are too. We both like swimming. Let's do it.'

'You're on,' he said.

Miss Murphy was mad about masks. The weeks before Easter, we had theory classes about the origin and development of masks. We had two classes then to make, paint and decorate a mask. She blocked us off so we couldn't see each other's work. The day before mid-term break, she said we should bring clothes to suit our masks. We would then try to guess who was who. She would also be part of the reveal.

I was Gandalf. My mask was a white face and grey beard. I created long grey hair from wool my mam gave me. My white cloak with hood was a large sheet with safety pins. Getting the staff proved difficult. Bamboo wasn't the thing. Dad called to Cassie's dad in the hardware shop and got a handle for a garden shovel. Job done.

We got dressed in the toilet cubicles. We all kept silent and arrived in the Art room to be met by weird and wonderful figures. I walked very straight, using my staff as if it were part of me. Around me, dresses swished, pirates romped, and Cinderellas abounded. Miss Murphy insisted on silence. She handed out sheets of paper and pencils. There were twenty of us. She handed us a number.

'Number one, step forward and walk around the room, please. Use a particular gait if you think that would help your character.'

We were asked to write down the students' names and characters. It was fascinating to see all the different masks and costumes. Number eight was easy to identify because Marcus Roche was the tallest boy in the class. Number twelve had to be Tracy English because she was tiny. I guessed the rest.

One character stood out. This person had taken their idea from Venetian carnivals. The face was pure white, with gold paint outlining the eye holes and mouth. The hair was covered in red velvet, above which rose a flower headdress. A green cloak covered the whole body and the back of the head. Long white cotton gloves completed the costume.

We held onto our paper, and then Miss Murphy

announced the unmasking. One by one, we emerged from behind our covers. The surprises! The laughter! The absolute admiration! We were amazed at our creativity.

But who was the student in the Venetian mask? It was Christopher, of course.

Miss Murphy gave him a book token for his efforts. She had snacks ready in the lunchroom. She took lots of photos. It was a wonderful day.

I still have the photo of the two of us on my bedroom wall – forever fourteen.

The end of May rolled around again, and the summer stretched ahead. Mam and Dad decided that Ellen and I should go to the Gaeltacht to improve our Irish. They would only let us go on a school-organised course. Christopher signed up as well. Howard needed no help with any language, but was still mooning over Ellen. I was sure Cassie would go, but she didn't.

All I could think of was Mr O'Gara and how he spoiled Fifth and Sixth classes for me. I hoped it wouldn't be like that. Miss Grayson was very good, and I liked to be in the 'sound centre'. My Irish would need to improve if I wanted to make a good showing in the Junior Cert.

It was a long way to Dingle, the bus took hours. Then, we were dropped off at various houses in Carraig, Feothanach, and Gallarus. We would attend classes in Muiríoch. We three lads were billeted in Carraig, close to the church. I wanted to know who I would share with. I wanted it to be Christopher, but Howard would also be fine.

I got both of them and a chap called Dessie Connaughton, who was a great singer. The room had two sets of bunks, and the space was limited. We tossed for the upper bunks. All four agreed that we would wash our feet before going to bed. Even with the window open, there was an odour.

Breakfast consisted of the caloga arbhair, tae agus aran (cornflakes, tea and bread). We headed off to walk to Muiríoch. En route, we met lots of the others heading our way. I spotted Ellen walking along with a girl I didn't know. We all walked together.

'That's my twin, Charlotte,' Ellen said.

'Hello all,' said the beautiful Charlotte.

Howard stayed where he was. I reckoned he thought his chances with Ellen were getting poorer by the minute. But school was school. We had grammar, reading, oral work and singing. By one o'clock, we were exhausted. We walked back to Carraig for dinner. Like a sensible person, Bean Ui Chronin had dinner in the middle of the day. We were not impressed with the mincemeat stew and despaired that it would be served to us several times a week.

We had no classes during the afternoons, but we weren't free. We went again to Muiríoch to spend the afternoon on the beach ag caint as Gaeilge (speaking Irish). The evenings were spent at a céilí, and were great fun.

Bean Ui Chronin served roast chicken, chips, peas and carrots the next day. She laughed and said the mincemeat stew the day before was a little trick she liked to play. So many women got a bad name for serving mince several times a week, that she and her friends decided it would never be said about them. She then shared a divine apple tart between the four of us.

The afternoons were a low point. The beach at

Muiríoch was stony, with seaweed covering the rocks and making progress slippery. Still, we were out of earshot of the monitoring teachers. As couples emerged, people drifted off for a walk along the beach. What they did behind the dunes was their own business.

Howard and Ellen were missing in action quite often. I thought she might get friendly with a new guy from another part of the country and broaden her outlook, but she and Howard seemed to have a genuine appreciation of each other. Did they have a lot in common? They were both very bright and could argue about the slightest thing. Howard wasn't the greatest looker, I'd say. With his long curls, glasses and wild t-shirts, he was nothing like Schooner. But how would I know what a girl would like about any guy?

Charlotte was left with us, but not every day. Ellen would sometimes head off with her. The three of us lads and Dessie Connaughton, our roommate, just laid out or skimmed stones. Poor Charlotte had no pal other than Ellen. We found ourselves acting like her older brothers.

Then, a day arrived when Ellen was off with Howard, and Charlotte went for a walk with Dessie. Christopher and I smiled.

'Here we are, left behind.'

'Suits me, Chris.'

'Suits you because the beloved Cassie is far away.'

'That is true. You see anyone you like?'

'Not an option. Don't want to give the goons from school any ammo.'

'Come on. We'll go to Ashe's shop and buy sweets as Gaeilge.'

On the Wednesday of the second week, lessons were cancelled. Bean Ui Chronin gave us a packed lunch, the bus collected us, and we spent a whole day touring the peninsula. In Dingle, we got bags of chips. The bus continued to Ventry, past Kruger Kavanagh's pub and Ballyferriter. The peaks of the Three Sisters pointed out to sea. It was ideal swimming weather. There was gold on the water and blue in the sky. We had the whole spread of the beach to ourselves. There were no stones, just beautiful silver sand and warm water.

Though we were dying to swim, we gave ourselves a few minutes to take it all in. The Three Sisters looked dramatic from this side. The three hills seemed to be running away to sea. Baile na nGall on the other side of the bay looked peaceful. Only a few fishing boats were tied up there, but Begley's pub was solid, close to the slipway.

We were in our togs in a flash. Howard and Ellen swam out a long way. Ellen was an excellent swimmer. Though she hated it when we were little, she took to swimming lessons like a duck to water. She was on the school swim team and loved sea swimming. I didn't even know that Howard could swim. He kept up with her, and they moved lazily out to the island.

Dessie and Charlotte set off together, but they didn't go out very far – they just lay down in the water and floated. They stayed close together, and I suspected there was more than hand-holding going on.

Christopher and I were in no rush. We had brought our snorkel gear. We ran in for a quick dip to get the feel of the water. It always takes your breath away. The ache of the cold only lasts a few seconds, but what a shock. Then comes the delight of the buoyancy and not having

A Boat for Benny

to swim, giving yourself to the water. We lay back and kicked our feet, barely paddling with our fingers.

It was time to get our snorkel gear.

'I'm going snorkelling by myself,' I said.

'Right so. I'll hang on here until you get back. Then you can do the same for me.'

I found my fins and snorkel, and I was ready. I waded out and attached the fins. Suddenly, I was seven feet long. I headed beyond the breakers to the calm zone, where I could see through clear water. The fronds of seaweed waved in slow motion. As the depth increased, I dived underwater and became accustomed to the cold and the colours. I moved long and easy, close to fronds, stones and sand. I searched the bottom for creatures and shells. Fish flashed before me, and crabs ran along the bottom. Sea anemones were few. Finding one was a delight. The world below the water line is a silent one. My ears were full of water, and I adapted to the silence. I might have been the only person in this sea at this time.

Eventually, the coldness got to me and dry land was calling. I came to the surface, flapped my fins and stretched my arms out, front-crawling the better to reach the shore. I was shivering like jelly.

'You're blue in the face and grey in the legs,' Christopher laughed.

'Off you go now to challenge the deep,' I said. 'Don't stay too long.'

I wrapped myself in a big towel and began to thaw out. I rubbed the towel all over me to get the circulation going. My shorts, t-shirt and hoodie made me warm.

I scanned the water for Christopher. I could see the splashes left by his fins, but then he dived. I waited for what seemed like an age.

We should have gone together. You're supposed to dive in pairs for fear of one person developing a problem. I had enjoyed snorkelling alone, and no harm had come to me. I was safely on the shore, but what if Christopher got into trouble? I waited for what seemed like an age. I saw the fins again as he lazily made his way back to the shore. My relief was huge.

'Who's blue and grey now?'

'Jesus wept, but it was so worth it.'

When we were both dry and dressed, he handed me a shell.

'That's for you to remember our day here.'

'You carried a shell back?'

'I have a pocket in my swim shorts.'

'You're a good lad. Do you know that?'

'Come on and pack your bag. Time we ate those sandwiches.'

There was still time to lie out and catch some rays.

'You're so lucky to have a twin.'

'Yes and no. I thought we would be alike because we were made together, but we're very different.'

'I know you have different interests, but you've known each other all your lives.'

'Before we were born, we were so close. Ellen did everything first. I was the follower.'

'I'm all on my own. You don't understand. I had no one to watch cartoons with on a Saturday morning, or go to the cinema in the afternoon. No one to share terrible jokes or pillow fights.'

I tried to imagine my life without Ellen. I couldn't. Though we had different personalities, likes and dislikes, there was an unseen, unspoken bond between us.

A Boat for Benny

'I can come over for a pillow fight anytime you like. I have a huge stock of really awful jokes, and I love the cinema. Take your pick.'

'Good call,' he said.

Christopher took the photo. There we were with the sea and Baile na nGall behind us, the three Sisters to our left and the dunes to the right. We drank Coke and laughed our hearts out. Our arms were around each other's shoulders, ready for anything life could throw our way.

The bus arrived, and the teachers blew whistles. We were in great form. After the tea, we would walk down to O'Shea's for uachtar reoite (ice cream).

Our Irish was lamentable when we arrived in Muiríoch, even though we had been learning it for ten years. In the space of three weeks, it had improved greatly. The reason was simple – we were not allowed to speak English, at least not within earshot of the teachers.

Céilí dancing? We knew nothing about that. Our dancing experience to date had consisted of school hops, music at birthday parties, and bedroom dancing to favourite tunes from Spotify. Céilí comes from the Irish words 'le cheile', meaning 'together'.

Our experience of céilí music was limited to short, quick bits from TV advertising or parades on St Patrick's Day. The first week, we had some basic classes at the school. Céilís were held on Tuesday, Thursday and Saturday nights.

Everything depends on one, two, three, one, two, three. Occasionally this would change to one, two, three, four, five, six, seven, but would always return to the one, two, three.

The main problem in learning Irish dancing is embarrassment. Everyone thought that everyone else was laughing at them; everyone worried that they were making a bigger fool of themselves than everyone else.

The boys formed a long line and had to hold the next boy's hand. We were reluctant, but the girls had no problem with it. On the spot, we tapped the right foot, made a small jump onto the left foot, and jumped back onto the right foot – we had our first one, two, three completed.

Then, a boy and a girl had to hold hands and repeat the steps. If that went fairly well, the pair now began dancing across. They did seven steps across, stopped and did one, two, three, one, two, three. They did seven steps back and then one, two, three twice more.

That is the essence of céilí dancing. Of course, there are different patterns, different types of swings, different numbers of partners and various tunes.

I had Howard on one side and Christopher on the other. Embarrassment was not a factor. Christopher certainly had more rhythm than Howard or me. While we struggled with the one, two, three, Christopher was picked to give a demonstration with Ellen. Several girls had learned Irish dancing as a hobby, so they had a head start on us.

Muinteor Maire put on a CD.

We stood in awe. They danced on the spot, to the side, back and on the spot again. She gave new instructions. They danced the basic step forward and back. Christopher took Ellen's elbow and swung her around. End of dance.

We clapped, and they smiled. Now, it seemed possible for all of us to improve.

There was dancing on the beach the first two afternoons. Though people fell, tripped over their feet and swung 'til they were dizzy, the fear had abated. On that first Tuesday night, we walked towards Begley's hall with determination, if not joy. We remembered it wasn't a case of jumping any old way and yelling. That first dance was the Siege of Ennis, the one we had been taught. We would have to learn the Walls of Limerick as well.

A lot of the girls caught on quickly, but some of the lads were challenged. It was all to do with hopping. If you could jump, you could learn.

As soon as we entered the hall, Mr Begley, the hall owner, gave a revision lesson on what we had done the first two days in school. At this stage, we knew the counting.

'Na feachaigi ar bhur gcosa,' Mr Begley called out. ('Don't look at your feet.')

Of course, he was right. You could manoeuvre yourself to the next spot if you looked at the people before you and forgot your feet. However bad we were by home time, we were much better than when we arrived.

Eight faced eight in the Siege of Ennis. Six steps in. Six steps back. The last girl in one row faces the last boy in the other row. They dance towards each other, swing around and return to their places. The opposite people then dance.

The four girls hold hands in the middle and dance in a circle. They go back. The four boys hold hands in the middle and then dance back. The eights hold hands and dance six steps in and back. Now, they dance six steps in again and pass through to the next set of eight. The Siege of Ennis could last for ages, depending on how many eights there were. You needed a rest afterwards, and a can of Coke or 7Up.

The band – two fiddles, a banjo and an accordion – took a rest. Everyone waited for the Old Time Waltz. For that, you could hold a girl. You could talk to her. You could even whisper to her if you wanted. There were lots of girls. We danced with Ellen and Charlotte but not for the waltzes. Charlotte gave Dessie all her waltzes, and there were no prizes for guessing who Ellen was with. I have a photo of Christopher and me doing a very decent whirl in a waltz. The smiles on our faces tell a good tale. Around the hall, girls and boys were dancing together. Christopher and I did not stick out as oddballs.

We sat down for a rest.

'You're really good at the dancing.'

'I went to lessons when I was small.'

I couldn't believe it!

'I thought it was only girls.'

'I used to have very round shoulders. Mam thought it would help me stand straight.'

'You'll have to give me a few lessons before we get home.'

'Why? Are you planning on keeping this up?'

'Stop laughing. Well, maybe a lesson or two here before the Céilí Mór on the last night. I want to dance the Siege of Ennis with Ellen just once.'

Dancing with a girl was lovely. Usually, they smelt of lemon shampoo or pleasant body wash. You hoped your deodorant was working because you would hate her to be assaulted by the smell of your dancing sweat.

Charlotte was lovely. I could relax dancing with

her as I wasn't trying to make an impression. She had a good sense of humour and a lovely smile. She and Dessie liked each other. They lived at opposite ends of the country, so saying goodbye would be hard.

Christopher and Ellen made a great partnership. They could really keep together and move smoothly. Lots of girls asked Christopher up, and he enjoyed the fun.

Promises were made about meeting in St Stephen's Green during the Halloween break. The four of us were happy to be heading home. We were bringing Muiríoch home with us in our memories and our photos.

I was excited to see Cassie, but she seemed indifferent to me. She and Ellen spent hours in Ellen's room, bringing each other up to date. They hardly noticed me.

'Ye seem to have had a great time, Benny,' Cassie said while we bought ice creams in Hogan's.

'It was great. I enjoyed being away from my parents, even though the teachers always watched us.'

'I'm just back a few days myself. Mam and I went to London for a week to visit my aunt. Benny, I went to the Tate Modern and the National Portrait Gallery.'

'You don't do Art,' I said, confused.

'I don't do it as an exam subject, but I love it, always have.'

We all hoped the last few weeks of August would bring glorious summer weather, since September would come soon enough. We wanted to squeeze every last drop out of the holidays: swimming in the lake, going for long cycles, lighting a bonfire in our garden, staying up very late, or not going to bed at all.

One night, the five of us slept under the stars in our garden. We had a small fire and cooked sausages. The fire smoke clung to our sleeping bags for days. The stars were magnificent. We tested ourselves on the constellations – or, rather, Howard tested the rest of us. We listened as he told the stories from the Greeks about the celestial formations. The dark is so important, he said. If you can see the dark sky, you can see a part of the universe we rarely explore.

Christopher and I went into overdrive about the night sky, and we searched online to learn more. Van Gogh's 'Starry Night' struck us dumb, so we listened to Don McLean's 'Vincent'.

I was lying on his bed, and he was at his desk.

'You won't believe it.'

'What?

'Come over and look at that. Vincent painted another Starry Night.'

I looked. This time, the stars were whirling over river water.

'It's called "Starry Night Over the Rhône".'

'I like it, but not as much as our starry night.'

We found Rembrandt's 'Night Watch', but there were no stars. We even looked at Georgia O'Keefe's 'Starlight Night'.

That night, I spoke to Dad about it all. 'Vincent' was written during Don's youth. Dad explained how popular it was and how many of his mates could sing all the lyrics. It was the story of Vincent's life, he said.

Mam joined us, and the pair of them told me about Don McLean's first hit, 'American Pie'.

'It made no sense,' Dad said. 'A single record that lasted eight minutes and thirty seconds had never been heard of.'

'Usually, a hit record would last three minutes,' Mam added.

He opened a press and took out the album American Pie. He lifted the lid on the record player, placed the precious plastic in position and said, 'Benny, this is music.'

FIVE

September arrived. We went off in our uniforms, carrying huge rucksacks full of books and tablets. The work was familiar as we continued the previous year's programme.

School demands took up our valuable time. Returning to uniform took away a lot of spontaneity from life and heralded the arrival of homework notebooks, past exam papers and the dreaded packed lunch.

Targets had to be met. In Woodwork, we learned new joints and lots of theory. For the practical section, we would have to make a bedside locker. For Art, we would also have to submit a piece. Needless to say, the Home Ec people would have to cook a sample meal.

Christopher's birthday arrived on October 4th. I was invited for tea. His parents were much older than Mam and Dad, but I knew them quite well by this stage. We had pizza with salad and then a fabulous birthday cake. The gifts he got were spot on. He got plenty of art materials, a hardback copy of To Kill a Mockingbird, a voucher for trainers, and a new phone.

We went to his room to look at the gifts and listen to music. A phone is a phone, but the quality of the camera is important for a photographer. His parents must have spent a fortune on the phone, because the camera on it was very advanced. I was impressed, even though all we did was make crazy faces and laugh at the pictures. I handed over my gift. I had rolled up my 'Boat at Sea' picture. It showed a vast but calm ocean. The sky was threatening. Moonlight drew your eye to a tiny boat alone in the void.

'So Benny, you painted a question. The sky will decide all the action. Thanks. It will always remind me of you.'

He hung it on the wall above his bed. I would have to wait 'til my birthday, months away, to discover what he had painted for me.

Halloween was coming up, and Miss Murphy brought the subject of masks up again.

'You have to do monochrome for your practical exam test. This would be a good chance to get it done. You don't have to stick with masks. The only rule is that your work must be in black and white.'

'But miss, we did masks last year.'

'Exactly, and everyone enjoyed that. Those sad French clowns are done in black and white, but you can choose any topic, any medium, but only in black and white. I do believe pandas are black and white. Prisoners' uniforms are sometimes black and white stripes. Anyway, those are the conditions. I will be marking it as part of your practical exam. I will give you two sessions in the computer room to do research. Enjoy.'

There had never been a revolution in the Art group before. Everyone liked Miss Murphy, and the mask business had been a great success. But this new project did not sit well with anyone. There were rumblings. If she noticed the lack of interest, she ignored it. We did the research. The overall feeling was that the French clowns were not funny. Most of them seemed to be sad, depressed even. They had painted-on tears and a melancholy air about them. They would never have been employed in a circus. Doing anything else in black and white sounded boring.

One class was enough to discover that everyone was against it. There was talk behind the sheds after school.

'She has always been approachable.'

'She has.'

'We loved the mask project last year.'

'We did.'

'Looking at the pictures of the French clowns just made me feel down.'

'What's to be gained by rehashing last year's idea? We gave it everything.'

Christopher had just listened to the conversation until this point, before saying, 'I'll talk to her. Let's face it, people, this is the first time we've had an issue.'

'Tell her we all feel the same.'

'I'll come with you,' I said.

'I'll go too,' said Caroline Brady.

We collared Miss Murphy in the Art room after school.

'Yes?'

'Miss, would you reconsider the monochrome project? We have no interest in doing it. You remember that last year's project engaged everyone. That won't happen this time.'

Her face immediately turned purple and red, like

a fuchsia flower.

'Well, how dare you!' she exclaimed, bursting into tears.

Tough, capable Miss Murphy dissolved into a weeping mess before our eyes.

'Tell you what,' she said through snuffles, 'forget the whole thing. I'll just mark everyone a C for monochrome.'

Christopher bristled. He knew his portfolio would have been worth an A. Caroline was a top student as well.

'That's not fair,' Christopher said.

'Tough toenails! Did anyone ever tell you life isn't fair?'

The silence was enormous. We left with our eyes down, treading lightly and feeling huge. Miss Murphy disappeared from school for two weeks, and we subsequently discovered she'd had a miscarriage. Oh, did we feel small!

The masks were unimportant compared to what Miss Murphy had been through. She had always treated us fairly and helped our self-esteem. When we thought it over, it was agreed that we had been too eager, too quick to complain, making our needs the only ones that mattered.

A delegation went to discuss the situation with Mr Finlay, and apologised for our behaviour. We said that we'd heard what had happened to her, and our remorse was genuine.

'I'm glad ye were mature enough to come to me. It certainly didn't help her. She lost twins, you see. Double the grief.'

Our faces hung long and pale in front of him. He

noticed our woebegone looks.

'Leave it now. Design a card and get all the Art students to sign it. That would be appreciated.'

I have a copy of the card here in my room. Of course, Christopher designed it. He wanted to create it in monochrome, but felt that might be like rubbing Miss Murphy's nose in it. Instead, he produced a drawing of his mask from the year before, with one large tear. We all signed it and wished her well. He got it photocopied for all of us.

SIX

We counted the days to mid-term break and decided we were too grown up to dress up for Halloween. Our plans for the mid-term break revolved around watching Halloween and its sequel, going to the Halloween hop and getting drinks.

Our house was the most amenable to lazy teenagers lolling on couches and eating all the bread. The usual suspects would arrive. We would order our pizzas, pay for them, and settle down to watch scary movies. Howard and Ellen were together on the two-seater. Cassie took the armchair. Christopher and I lay on the floor with cushions under our heads. We had the lights off. Only the glow from the screen kept us from total darkness.

Ellen brought cans from her room. Cassie got vodka from her rucksack. Mam and Dad were due back at eleven. We started on the beer, but Cassie immediately went for the vodka. The things you don't know about people! I kept an eye on Cassie in the gloom. She was well able for the vodka. It was the first time I had seen her drinking.

'Take it handy there, Cassie,' Ellen said. 'You don't want Mam and Dad to see you under the influence.'

'They'll think I'm just drinking Coke. That's what

they think at home.'

I thought the beer was a bit soapy and didn't like the taste. I slowed down because I was keeping an eye on Cassie. Everyone was chilled out, and hearing the actor pronouncing Samhain 'sam-hain' made us roll around laughing.

I thought Christopher and I should walk Cassie home.

'Am I a child? I'm perfectly capable of getting home on my own,' she replied.

Ellen nodded, and we headed off. She nearly fell. I held one elbow, and Christopher had the other.

'You'll be in trouble. Your folks will know you're not sober.'

'They're away overnight. I can do what I like.'

We waited until she opened the front door, and I walked on with Christopher.

'She's in a bad way,' he said.

'I had no idea. Beer is one thing, but vodka! That's serious.'

'She must be on it a while. She knows all the tricks.'

'I don't know. She's in our house a lot of the time. She and Ellen are as thick as thieves. I haven't noticed anything before.'

'Is she on her own in her house a lot?'

'I haven't a clue. Her dad's in the shop, and her mam does the accounts in the house.'

'It's a worry for you.'

'What do you mean?'

'Benny, I know what I know. You're crazy about her.'

I said not one word, but he was right.

I turned back at his house. The light was on in

Cassie's bedroom. I was worried, but I could do nothing about her safety. I wanted to mind her, listen to her and help if I could.

I tackled Ellen the next day. She gave me a blank look. I knew she knew some of the story, but prodding it out of her was impossible.

'She was half-drunk when we got to her house.'

'Did you go in?'

'Why would I go in? She closed the door very quickly. What good would I have been? Her parents are away until tomorrow. She should be sober by then.'

'She has things on her mind. I do my best. I like a few cans, but the vodka is bad news. It could be worse. She could be on drugs.'

As if I didn't have enough to worry about. Jesus wept!

She clammed up then.

Cassie did not appear at our house over the next few days. I did a few hours in the garage for Dad. On Tuesday night, the Halloween Hop took place in the Snooker Club hall. It wasn't an official school hop, so Mr Conroy would not be on door duty. Christopher and I sauntered up together. There were supervisors, but they weren't teachers. A few of the club members were chatting together. They did not seem to understand that they should have had their eyes open, skimming the hall.

Supervising a teenage hop requires experts – one's sight and hearing have to be engaged at all times. They have to know the signs of aggro before it ever happens. There must be female supervisors as well as male, since the toilets need checking frequently.

Pockets or handbags weren't checked, and WhatsApp was busy as those in the hall informed those en route that they could get vodka, gin or a fix through without a problem.

The designated bouncers were just tokens, ordinary guys who we all knew by sight. They had never stood outside a pub or a club after midnight on a weekend.

The girls were in a big group, dancing together in a huddle. Cassie looked gorgeous. She was wearing tight jeans with a pale blue top. Her hair was hanging all around her face. Howard was keeping an eye on Ellen, who didn't give him even a glance. She was in a pair of shorts with black tights underneath and a tiny vest. She had high-laced boots I had never seen before.

'Oh my God, Ellen looks fantastic,' he croaked.

'Watch your business,' I said. 'She's one in a million.'

'You're raving about Cassie. I can say what I want to say.'

When the music changed to a slow set, Ellen made a beeline for Howard and threw her arms around his neck. I saw Cassie and asked her to dance. We moved awkwardly as I didn't know how to do anything except one to the left and one to the right.

She was very quiet, but then she burped. We headed outside, and she threw up over my good shoes and new jeans. Her face was a ghostly white, and she shivered. Two lads out for a smoke brought me a damp towel from the bathroom. I cleaned her up, wiped my shoes and decided to take her home. She was belligerent and cross.

The sound of The Proclaimers' '500 Miles' was pulsing out into the night. The floor shook with them all jumping and singing the 'duh, duh, duh, duh,' and waving their hands at the chorus. I felt sorry for myself, missing all the fun. I knew that Christopher's hair would be flying as he jumped around, because he loved that song.

Cassie was slurring her speech as she talked to herself all the way. I had to keep my arm around her waist to keep her vertical and walking.

'I'll bring you to our house for coffee. That will sober you up a bit.'

'I want to go home.'

'You can't go into your parents' house in that state. Come with me.'

'Benny, bring me home.'

So, I did.

'Thank you for helping me. Goodnight.'

'I'll come in and make you some coffee.'

'I've only had a few drinks. Keep your hair on.'

There was nothing else. It might be good if her parents saw her in this state. They would know what was going on.

I walked home, hardly noticing the starry night or the quietness around me. There was no point in going back to the hop.

Mam came into my room early, sitting on the bed and shaking me awake.

'Wake up, Benny. There's been an accident.'

In an instant, I was wide awake, my brain alert, and messages flying around my head.

'Is she alright?'

'Who?'

'Cassie.'

'Nothing's wrong with Cassie. It's Christopher.'
I looked at her then.
'He was knocked down on the way home from the hop.'
'Is he alright?'
'Justin, Justin – come here for God's sake.'
Dad arrived.
'He's not alright. He has severe head injuries, Benny. He's on life support.'
Mam sobbed.
'My heart is breaking for his parents. Imagine the shock of it. And being told that there is no hope of his recovery. Oh, God help them.'
Dad spoke very quietly.
'Benny, son, how come you weren't with him?'
This was no time to be coy or cute.
'I walked home with Cassie because she was feeling sick.'
'Was it sick or vodka-sick?' asked Mam, who knew everything.
'Who cares, Mam? Christopher is going to die.'
'You should go to the hospital and see him. His mother said you were welcome to go down. No one else is allowed in, just his parents and you.'
'It was a hit and run. He was left on the road. A few snooker chaps found him, but too much time had passed. He lost a lot of blood.'
'You mean he could have been saved if he had been found earlier?'
'I can't answer that, Benny.'
I could feel the anger rise in me.
'They hadn't a clue how to run a hop. The bouncers were useless. They didn't check pockets or handbags.

A Boat for Benny

Drink and drugs made their way in, no problem.'

Mam drove me ten miles to the big town. I walked towards the hospital. The world just kept on turning – people walked by with the newspaper under their arms, some ducked into the betting office while others drank coffee in cafés.

My friend was dying, and the world just went on.

I thought about Seamus Heaney's poem 'Mid-Term Break'. His small brother, aged only four, was knocked down and died – 'A four-foot box / A foot for every year.'

Now my Christopher was leaving too. I had to see him. It's what human beings do. They say goodbye to the one who is going into the other room. I had heard the words, but I didn't believe them. I had seen him the night before. I had whispered to him about Cassie being ill.

'Go home with her,' he had said. 'Get her safely home. I'll see you tomorrow.'

I hadn't been there, and he hadn't got home safely.

They were all wrong. Of course they were. If he were in a coma, he would come out of it. People sometimes come out of them after years spent unconscious.

It was quiet in the room. Yes, there were machines, but they were rhythmic and calming, if you can believe that. I looked at his mother and father. I was afraid to look at my boy. His mam took my hand and placed it on his. He was warm, and I stroked the back of his hand. His face was grey. His blond hair was clipped back from his forehead. He would have hated that, but he was beyond all feelings now.

He lay sleeping with machines keeping him alive. Same face, same hair, same thin fingers, but no smile.

I held his hand. I spoke silently to him. I told him it was all a mistake. The doctors were waiting for him to wake up. He would be fine. He would walk and talk again and be his old self.

I couldn't believe that he might die. I thought of how people wake up from comas. I reminded myself how disoriented I had been when I fell off my bicycle. I waited for a flicker from his eyelids. The hum of the machines continued. Numbers appeared on the monitors, but they meant nothing to me. I held his hand. His fingers were long and thin, piano players' fingers. I recalled how he would hold charcoal while sketching, firmly but easily. Charcoal never broke in Christopher's hand.

'When will he wake up?' I asked his mam.

'He won't wake up, Benny. The machines are doing all the work.'

'Can they not do anything?'

'No, Benny. He can't even breathe on his own. We have a few days before the machine is turned off.'

'But I have so many things to say to him! We were making plans for our portfolios. I'll never manage on my own. What will I do?'

A sob escaped from his mother, before his dad put his arms around her.

'I can't take it in. I'm waiting for him to wake up,' Eithne said.

The nurse suggested that they go and have some breakfast.

'I'll mind him,' I said.

I held both of his hands.

'What will I do without you, Chris? What about the picture of the ship on the sea? My birthday isn't

A Boat for Benny

for ages. I'll never get it now. You'll never take all the pictures you had planned on your new phone. Sorry. I'm going to shut up now and listen to you.'

I fancied I could see movement under his eyelids. I felt the pulse at his wrist.

'No more cross-country running for you, boy, unless they race in heaven.'

I listened to myself and knew that I sounded like an idiot. I sat and cried. You know the quiet crying that grows a massive lump in your throat, and it feels like you're choking? I was making no sense to myself. I certainly wasn't making sense to my friend in the bed. I pulled out The Catcher in the Rye and read it aloud to him.

His parents came back, and the nurses needed to do their work.

'May I come back tomorrow?'

'Of course you can, Benny.'

'Could you bring in To Kill a Mockingbird, the copy he got for his birthday? I want to share some of that with him, even if he can't hear me.'

'Oh, he did admire Scout. I mean, does,' his dad said.

They each lay across him and took his hands. I slipped out.

Our town was in shock. They opened the school so that students could gather and talk to each other. Father Darmody said Mass in the hall. I didn't go; I went home. Mam was there, as were Ellen and Howard. We just sat, listening to the clock ticking – time seemed to be on a go-slow.

'How did he look?' Ellen ventured.

'Warm but very pale. He looked asleep. I could

hold his hand. They left me alone with him, and I read to him. I'm going back tomorrow.'

Tears rolled down my face.

'No more painting or taking pictures. It's not fair. He's one of the good guys.'

'Was he in our class in primary school?' Howard asked.

'He was, but we didn't know him then. He remembered Miss Atkins and the play.'

'What part did he have?'

I burst out laughing, and found myself near-hysterical.

'He was a star but didn't appear as he was at home sick. The show went on without one star. What will I do without him?' I asked.

Nobody knew.

I read the piece from To Kill a Mockingbird to him, the bit where Atticus stays in the jail all night in case someone came to hurt Tom Robinson. We had talked so much about Atticus and how his attitude towards black people differed from the run-of-mill ideas that still existed in the South. I sat close to him, held his hand and spoke close to his ear. I could feel him slipping away. The machines still worked; they sounded familiar to me now, but I could feel a change.

I didn't want him to go. I wanted him to sit up in bed and say, 'Jesus wept! I have a shocking headache.'

'Come on, kid,' I whispered. 'You can't go. We have to grow up and be men together. This is only the start. We have so many plans. Don't you remember?'

His parents came in. Immediately, the dad left again to call the doctor. Soon, the machines made different sounds, and the staff worked and worked on him.

'Turn off the machine now, Andy. Let him drift away in peace.'

They took out the ventilator tube. Soon, there was no rise and fall at his chest. The machine beeped a flatline. Christopher was gone.

I wanted to fly away. It's a primitive response to dangerous situations. Early people had a choice – they could stand and fight the wild animal threatening them, or they could run as fast as they could. Christopher had never been a threat to me, quite the opposite. His stillness put me into overdrive. I wanted to flee. I began to make my way out, but Eithne stopped me.

'Say goodbye to him, Benny. His gentle spirit is leaving.'

I had to stay. I held his hand, which was already cooling. I whispered into his ear, 'Don't you dare leave me. However you can manage, come back.'

We stood around him and cried. His parents put their arms around me. I put my arms around Christopher and whispered, 'My brother.'

I didn't want to go. The next time I would see him would be in a coffin. A bed is the right place for a person, even when they're dead.

The room became cold. Shivers ran down my back. My breaths came in big gulps, as if I was fighting for air. My head was whirling, and my legs started to shake. His parents were crying quietly. I felt the tears course down my face. Something shifted in my chest. I recognised the pain as a loss – a huge loss.

I left. I picked up the book on my way. Mam was

waiting for me. She knew by my face that the worst had happened. As soon as she hugged me, I wailed. She stopped the car and let me get it out. She ended up crying herself.

'I liked Christopher. He was a great friend to you.'

'He was the best,' I said. 'I'm not able to put it into words. We suited each other. He was like my brother.'

'You have a good heart, Benny. A really good heart.'

I cried again.

'Mam, he was my brother. I loved him.'

We were silent the rest of the way home. Howard and Ellen met us in the hall. She hugged me so tight and sobbed hard. Howard said, 'I'm so sorry, Benny.'

The next few days were a blur. They waked him at home. People came to see and pray for the corpse. Candles cast a gentle glow all over the room. Christopher lay in his coffin wearing a black shirt and his leather jacket. I felt sure he had the good black trousers and the elegant black leather brogues he kept for good wear. People moved on to the kitchen while more arrived. The neighbours were busy making tea and offering whiskey. Discreet knocks on the back door meant the arrival of more apple tarts, sandwiches and bottles of wine.

Eithne and Andy sat and spoke to the people. They told the story over and over, not missing a detail. They spoke about what a great son he was and how blessed they were to have him. I didn't hear much because I was in and out of the sitting room. Christopher's aunts, uncles and cousins had arrived from the West and Wicklow.

Mam and Dad came. She cried. All the evenings

and nights he had spent in our house had made him one of the family. She had noticed how happy I was to have such a good friend, one brought the best out in me.

From the kitchen, I could hear her crying again.

'God help you, Eithne.'

'We're heartbroken.'

'He was a great lad. We knew him well.'

'He loved going to your place. He had Benny and the others as well.'

They moved off. Other people came into the kitchen and were fed.

So many people from school arrived – I was quite surprised. A wake is traditional, observed mainly by older people. I had my seat close to him and nodded as mourners came. Girls were weeping and holding on to each other. Several lads from 3B were morose and shook hands with me. Whether they entered the kitchen or left through the front door, I cannot say. Miss Murphy cried. She told Eithne he had great talent and would have made a fine artist. Mr Fennessy spoke about his love of wood and his immaculate work.

Part of the ritual of the wake is to stay awake with the corpse through the night. A small group stay in the room, the candles are maintained, prayers are said aloud, and tea and spirits are drunk. At three a.m., the place fell silent. People show honour to the dead in many ways, silence being one of them. At about four, I played Cat Stevens and George Harrison, two of Christopher's favourite artists. There was no clip in his hair. He was as still as stone. Once the dawn lit the sky, I left and got a few hours of sleep.

The funeral would leave the house at ten o'clock.

A crowd waited outside. The howls from Eithne and Andy as the coffin was closed were pure pain. She began to scream. He held her up because she could not stand on her own. Her sister was at her elbow.

I walked behind the hearse. Howard, Ellen and Cassie were with me. People joined the cortege up the town. There was a guard of honour from the school.

The coffin was wheeled in, flowers covering it. The Mass began. It was a tribute to Christopher's life and talent. Andy's people supplied the music. The fiddle played, and the flute, concertina and banjo picked up the tune. Christopher's aunt sang.

I did nothing. I didn't read a prayer or bring up an offertory gift. I wasn't in the group that brought up symbols of his life. Ellen brought up my picture of the boat at sea, and Howard brought up his phone. I was doing fine until the offertory procession. The cousin stood at the ambo. She began to sing 'Be Not Afraid', and I managed to keep my feelings under control until she came to the words, 'Be not afraid / I go before you always'.

He would never go before me again. My life would be lived without him beside me, behind me, above or below me. We would never swim together, take pictures, draw, paint or work with wood. There would be no more discussions about novels, Shakespeare or artists. Christopher had left me all alone.

I don't know how Andy did it, but he gave a beautiful eulogy. He spoke about how lucky they were to have Christopher. They were both in their forties when they married. What incredible luck that Christopher arrived. He even mentioned me.

A Boat for Benny

Putting him into the ground was rough. There is no avoiding the hole, the heap of clay and the fact that Christopher would be left there. None of his forebears are buried here. Then I thought of my grandad and Granny Mac. Though they're on the other side of the cemetery, they will surely call over to see that he is settled.

It's different when old people die. No matter how much you love them, they have lived a lifetime by the time grandchildren get to know them. My grandad was the best. He had a great sense of humour and told brilliant stories. He had a workshop out the back and made a go-kart for Ellen and me. His hands were full of veins that stuck out like railway tracks. He didn't walk so fast, and sometimes had a drip at the end of his nose.

He got sick. He couldn't remember things. He said it was morning when it was time to go to bed. He shouted and said Mam was starving him. He couldn't remember that he had eaten his breakfast. He accused Dad of stealing money from him. He had no peace as the dementia took him over, and left only traces of our wonderful Papa.

At Grandad's funeral, I didn't feel comfortable. Granny and Mam cried. He was laid out in the sitting room. The people came and shook hands. We walked up to the church and left him there overnight. The next day, we put him in the ground. He was with a lot of dead people that he knew in life. Even his parents were there. We left him there feeling sad and relieved – sad he was gone, but relieved he would be tormented no more.

'Will you explain this new money to me, Benny?'

he had asked one day.

He was lost after a few seconds. Within a minute, he had forgotten what he had asked me. It's called 'the long goodbye'. Bits of Grandad drifted away over a long time, and when he passed, he was only a shell of himself.

But Christopher did not get sick. In a split second, his life was snuffed out by someone who was in no fit state to drive. I had admired Christopher's courage. Christopher had accepted himself and didn't try to be anything else. He talked about going to Trinity and studying Pure English – that always made me smile. You haven't heard of Pure Geography or Pure Accountancy. You don't even think about Pure Art. He chortled when I said this to him.

'Stop, Benny. You're killing me.'

I had a smile to myself, but then I started to cry because I would never make him laugh again.

'You have a unique sense of humour, Cullen.'

He was unique with his slow walk and cool blond hair. When Christopher left, some of the bright colours went out of my life. He and I understood each other. If my dreams came true, he would have helped me choose an engagement ring for Cassie.

I couldn't face the lunch in the hotel, but Mam and Dad went. I walked home. I was trying to get through to heaven telepathically, but the lines must have been very busy. All I got was interference.

Cassie caught up with me.

'Benny, you would have been with him if it hadn't been for me – he would still be here.'

'You can't think like that. I had texted him to say I was bringing you home.'

'Well, it's all out now. Everyone knows about me and the vodka.'

'I hope you'll sort yourself out, Cassie. But right now, I need some peace.'

Ellen and Howard were there before us and ordered food. We watched Batteries Not Included and Toy Story and ate burgers and chips. I fell asleep during Toy Story. They watched on. They were minding me. No one had been minding Chris on his way home.

I imagined him dossing along, singing under his breath and deciding what to wear the next day. He was a cool dresser. He favoured black shirts and black chinos. He liked his black leather coat. With his hair flowing down his back, he was a one-off. Designer.

SEVEN

Ellen looked after me. She watched me all the time. For a few nights, I slept on the floor in her room. I didn't have to ask. She put a groundsheet, my pillow and duvet beside her bed.

'Stay for a few nights. We started off together, so you might need me close because you're so hurt and miserable.'

I was surprised, shocked and grateful. Most of the time, I felt that I was just her brother. I used to believe that twins possessed some special closeness together. I thought we should have had a subconscious connection, something like telepathy. I had read about twins who could finish each other's sentences, anticipate something that would happen to the other, and even feel physical pain when their twin was hurt. Nothing like that had ever happened between us.

From the time other children entered our lives, the drift apart began. I wanted to keep following her, be her number-one playmate and swimming companion.

Having to go to different primary schools was the killer blow. It was natural to gravitate towards the human beings in your class and play with them. Even I couldn't survive by waiting to go home to see Ellen. I had to fill my time with boys, the only humans available.

A Boat for Benny

Cassie's presence in our house was constant. The girls ran upstairs and settled in Ellen's room. Hoots of laughter filled the top of the house. Once I opened the door, Ellen shouted, 'Get out. Get out, this is a boy-free zone.'

After that, she put a sign on the door to that effect, with a skull and crossbones on it.

I wasn't afraid, but I could see that I wasn't wanted. Cassie was always welcome, it seemed. In recent times, that welcome had been extended to Howard. I kept well away from the place myself.

My misery had touched her well-hidden heart, and I was grateful. I thought I wouldn't sleep a wink, but I was wrong. Though the curtains let in more light than my own and the groundsheet was flat and uncomfortable, I drifted off easily. I could hear Ellen's breathing, which soothed me. One night, I woke up crying. She said nothing but reached her hand down and held mine.

After a week, I decided to go to my own bed.

'Anytime you need company, just bring your sleeping bag in.'

'Thanks, I will. I needed that help, and you gave it to me.'

'Enough, enough, Benny. No big deal – arrive if you need to. Who knows? Someday, you might have to do the same for me.'

If Howard arrived, she hardly noticed him. Cassie walked to the library with me and Howard played computer games. I was more like a zombie than a player, but he tolerated me.

Mam and Dad watched me constantly. I could hear them talking in their room. Dad spoke to me about loss and grief, but it all flew over my head. Mam said I could tell her anything.

What I wanted to say was, 'There's a lump of ice in my chest, which makes breathing difficult. I'm afraid to go to sleep in case I die. If I do sleep, I see him lying in the coffin. I want to phone him, FaceTime him, hang out in his room and eat the lasagne he cooked. I want him back in this house for Friday evenings with the chip dinner. I want to go snorkelling again as we did in Kerry. I even want to do céilí dancing with him. My heart is breaking.'

But I didn't.

Safety! I had my bed, books, drawings and photos of Christopher and me. But there was no sign of him, no sign of my fabulous, brilliant boy. I would never see him again.

Monday came, and the mid-term break was over. Life went on. In fairness, we weren't attached at the hip. We only had two option subjects that were the same, and we loved English. I knew that was my practical brain trying to control how I felt. This was tossing him aside as if he was of no consequence. That voice in my head was alien.

Can you reduce a friendship to these kinds of labels? I think not. Our time in and out of school was spent together. We didn't have to speak. We could sit and read without opening our mouths. In their sitting room, they had two big couches. We could lie down, stretch out, put cushions under our heads and get on with pure reading.

We talked about Goodnight Mister Tom. We found it inspiring but also full of sadness and cruelty.

He loved sonnets, too, once saying to me, 'Benny, a sonnet is a work of art.'

'It's fourteen lines of some guy being smart with the rhyme.'

'It's the world condensed in literary form.'

'They're easy to learn off, I grant you.'

'You ask your mam and dad. I bet they remember sonnets from their schooldays.'

He had been right – for they did remember them and longer poems, too.

'Well, what about "Ozymandias"?'

'Easy peasy. If you build huge monuments to show how powerful you are, you imagine they will last forever. Time and desert sands combine to knock them over and cover them. Such pride is foolish.'

I thought about that conversation. He was gone in an instant. He didn't get the time to become a grown man, never mind an old man. No doubt, as time passed and I got better at English, I would relate better to the sonnet. But right then, the only line that made sense was 'nothing beside remains'.

I missed him at lunchtime. We had a favourite spot in the canteen. Cassie, Howard and Ellen made sure I wasn't on my own. Walking home alone was hard. Cassie waited, said nothing and joined in with me.

'I want to talk to you.'

'Okay.'

'I want to explain something.'

'No need. I washed my shirt and cleaned my shoes. No explanation needed.'

'My dad is having an affair.'

That stopped me. She had a sad, demoralised look on her face.

'He's shagging that new chiropractor. She's in the church choir with him.'

'How do you know?

'They were in the Wishbone last Friday night. I saw them in her car down by the convent. I swear he was riding her in the front seat. Wouldn't that turn anyone to drink?'

Reality is cold. It crawls up your sleeves and around your neck. It gives you shivers. I already had too much in my head, and this news only added to my uncertainty. Her dad was still alive, but Christopher was gone – he can't breathe, make blood, pump his heart, or even smile.

'I suspected it for a while. He's never had an issue with his back. A few months ago, he started complaining. My poor mother made an appointment for him with the new chiropractor. Next, we heard the chiropractor had joined the choir. He's still attending her for his back. In fairness, Benny, I don't think it's his back. They're having sex.'

'Does your mam know anything?'

'The poor innocent hasn't a clue. She meets your woman, Mavis, for coffee. She says she's helping the stranger to feel part of the community. Sometimes, I want to scream at her, "She's part of the community already, Mam. She knows Dad intimately".'

'Ah, Cassie, that's terrible.'

'If I say nothing, I'm keeping Mam in the dark, and that's not fair. If I tell Mam, there will be warfare. I'm sticking my head in the sand, I know. That's why a drink or two is so handy. It dulls my brain, and I can sleep at night. It helps me get through the pain.'

I understood clearly. The pain of losing Christopher

was like a lead ball in my stomach. I knew very well that this time after the funeral was unreal. I didn't tell her I had to stop texting him that morning. I had forgotten that he was dead.

'Maybe we can help each other through this sad time, Cassie.'

'She's one of those women who beguile men. Do you know what I mean? They look deeply into a man's eyes, even if he only talks about the weather. Dad thinks all his birthdays have come at once. It makes me sick.'

'It might fizzle out in a few weeks. No need to upset your mam for now.'

'The choir is going to Rome for a beatification next month. Mam's staying at home with me.'

'They're not stupid enough to be caught doing anything by the choir members or Father Darmody.'

'I'd say half the choir know already.'

'Leave it now. Come to our house for tea.'

I was walking along with my hands in my trouser pockets. I felt a little hand join mine. I took out my hand and held hers. I didn't even look at her. I'd never held a girl's hand before, and it felt good. We didn't need to speak. We both felt safe. I did, anyway.

They were all there. Dad was up from the garage, Mam was knitting and Howard and Ellen were watching TV. I made tea, and we carried our mugs up to my room. If people thought it was strange, I didn't care. I sat on my bed, and she sat on my chair.

'It thumps in my head all the time,' she said. 'When I have a drink, the pain eases.'

'You're trying to deal with something too big for you. It's an adult problem.'

'You're coping with an adult issue. Fifteen-year-olds are not supposed to die, ever. Death should be very far away for us. Grannies and grandads, yes, but best friends, no.'

'I'm so lonely without him. Even in Art and Woodwork, we were a team.'

'I can't believe what's happened to my parents, my poor Mam.'

I thought then of how long I had liked this girl. But now I had too much on my mind to even consider her problem. We were just two teenagers in trouble. I didn't want to hold her or kiss her. I wanted her to go away and leave me alone. Another time, I might not feel so low and would be able to listen. Today, I had no empathy for anyone. I could only feel my loss, and it was tremendous.

'When the shit hits the fan, can I depend on you, Benny?'

'When I'm down, can I depend on you, Cassie?'

'Deal,' she said.

'Done deal,' I said.

I walked as far as the bridge with her. It was easy to say I would be there for her, but my own problem was so large it blocked out everything else. When I got home, they were all quiet.

'The whole town knows what's going on,' Mam said.

'I don't know anything about anything,' Dad said, nonplussed.

Ellen tried to act innocent, but she knew.

'Cassie's dad is having an affair with the new chiropractor.'

Dad nearly exploded.

A Boat for Benny

'He's having an affair with that one who sings in the choir with him?'

'God help Anna, she hasn't a clue. She was being nice to the stranger, inviting her for coffee. They've been seen in the woman's car.'

Dad's face was contorted. He was trying to imagine intimacy in a car at his age.

By the time Cassie got home, her mam knew. She had been getting his suit ready to go to the cleaners. In the jacket pocket, she found the receipt for the Wishbone and one for the hotel in the next town.

He moved into the woman's apartment within the hour, and moved back home the next day. The chiropractor had thrown him out.

EIGHT

Cassie decided she couldn't stay at home while her parents were at war. She gave it a week, but the air was poison. She came to our house for a break. You have to laugh. I was grieving for my best friend, but Ellen was her best friend. Where else would she go? She and Ellen slept in Ellen's room, sharing a bed. I could hear them giggling at night.

Girls have no difficulty sleeping beside their best friends. I suspect they can even cuddle up to each other as well. In a million years, guys wouldn't do that. I'd sleep on Christopher's floor quicker than I would share a bed. Not because he is gay but because we are lads. Wrong tense, Benny. Now, I wouldn't sleep beside him because he is dead.

Christmas was coming ever closer, and it filled me with dread. I thought of Chris's parents and how morbid their Christmas would be. I considered how far I was from 'tidings of comfort and joy'. If there had been a vote, I would have chosen to cancel Christmas this year.

But it went ahead anyway.

We had an easy slide into December as we would be doing mock exams in the New Year. Instead, we were asked to work in the community during school hours. You could join the carol singers and tour the town. Another choice was to collect items for the Lions Club at Tesco and Supervalu. The items would make up hampers for those in need. I chose to help older people put up their Christmas tree. I would have wanted Christopher as a partner. I could imagine the fine job he would do. He had an eye for style and design.

Mr Flavin insisted that we go in pairs. He put me with a new girl who had just arrived from Donegal. It didn't matter. Christopher was gone. Anyone else would just be making up the numbers.

Mrs McDermott lived near the nun's chapel. In we went.

'Who would you be now?'

'I'm Benny Cullen. My dad runs the garage.'

'Ah, I have you now. And your mother knits for people.'

'She does.'

'And yourself, do I know you at all?'

'I'm Hetty. I only arrived a few weeks ago.'

'I heard what happened to your friend. I'm sorry,' she said, looking at me.

I wanted the ground to open up and swallow me. Of course, everyone in the town knew. I didn't want a stranger to know my business, but the damage was done.

'We'll have a cup of tea,' said Mrs Mc, 'and then we'll get to work.'

I usually love scones, but these were like balls of wool on my tongue. The woman and the girl chatted away as if they knew each other. I was like the one who had recently arrived.

Sorting the tree involved moving a sideboard to the dining room. Then, we had free rein. The woman sat on the couch and directed operations.

Some of her decorations were beautiful, and others were ancient. They were handmade when her children were young. Everyone has samples in their own house. Mam has a paper lantern I made in First Class, a Santa made of cotton wool with one eye, and a purple Jesus coloured in by Ellen. We tried tucking the old decorations in at the back, but Mrs Mc was having none of it.

'I want to be able to see the little lamb. Michael made that. Move the star up to where it should be. I know the glitter is nearly all gone, but Susan took hours to make it.'

I wondered what handmade bits Chris's parents would use. Would they put up a tree at all? They had nothing to celebrate. Cassie's family were in a bind as well.

When we had finished, we took a selfie with Mrs Mc, since Mr Flavin would need proof that we had done the work.

The following day, Mr Flavin got a call from an old man who wanted us to put up his tree. In we went.

'We'll start straight away,' we said. 'Where's the tree?'

'Ah, no. We'll have a cup of tea first.'

To be polite, we had to have the tea. He put out Bourbon Creams.

'You can get them for 24 cents in Aldi, but I always buy Jacob's. My mother bought Jacob's, as did my wife, and I wouldn't change.'

He talked on. He told us about his garden and his

A Boat for Benny

plans for the spring, which potatoes he would sow, and how he would try carrots again even though the carrot fly was rampant in the area.

'Right, Mr O'Brien, we should get started.'

'There's no tree,' he said. 'I get very lonely here on my own, so I told a little white lie. I wanted a bit of company, that's all. We had a wonderful tree when my wife was alive, but I've nothing to celebrate since she passed.'

We left.

'I'm getting that man a tree,' Hetty said.

'My dad will pay for a set of lights,' I said.

'We'll explain it all to Mr Flavin, and see if the class can give a few decorations,' Hetty said.

Mr Flavin had a chat with the Head. Hetty explained to the class what we needed. We got lights, decorations, a crib and candles.

Mr O'Brien let us in, and we told him straight out what we'd done, before bringing all the stuff inside.

The sitting room had a large window, and we placed the tree in front of it. We sent Mr O to the kitchen while putting the finishing touches on the work. We brought him in to see the switch on. He was thrilled. He cried then and said, 'A bit of the Christmas feeling might come back to me now.'

'The carol singers will be around and will stop outside your window. Keep the curtains open so that you will hear us,' Ellen said.

'I'll be calling with a Christmas hamper with lots of nice goodies,' Cassie added.

That night I lay in bed, pleased that Hetty and I had brightened up Mr O'Brien's Christmas. A familiar voice could be heard from the top of the wardrobe.

Could it be?

'There you go. You thought about someone else today instead of pining over me.'

'Christopher, are you here?

'Let's just say I'm keeping an eye on you. The powers that be say I was wrenched away too young. They're giving me a bit of a reprieve.'

'You're welcome back, so welcome. I want to see you.'

'Benny, you can hear me. That will have to be enough. The message is that when you put other people first, you stop being consumed with yourself.'

'I miss you so much.'

'And I miss you. Just don't torture yourself with what-might-have-been.'

'You were my best buddy.'

'What's this "were" business? I am your best buddy.'

'Where are you, Christopher?'

'I'm between worlds for now. In fairness, it suits me very well. It's an art room with woodwork tools. It's a section for teens only. People from all over the world, boy. Here's the secret. No matter a person's language, you hear their words in your own language. Imagine. I can understand Mandarin and Hindi!'

'Sounds ideal for a guy like you.'

'Benny, you have to be dead to get here. We are in transition. It's all new. But I miss my folks, and I miss you.'

I needed to hear that. I felt like spilling all my feelings to him. I wanted to howl with misery and show him my broken heart.

'Listen, I want you to have my phone. You know how good the camera is.'

A Boat for Benny

'Let's see. Your folks need all the signs of you near them and will for ages. If you're filling my head, imagine their state of mind.'

'This idea of the soul leaving the body is untrue. I was at my own funeral. Would you believe that? I saw and heard everything. Once the coffin was lowered, I left. Two policemen drove me to where I am now. It's like a huge plane hangar for all the world. There's a swimming pool and games room. I've been painting a lot. Hammocks hang everywhere. We sleep in them at night. We have to regain our strength after the big trip. They're cleaning our lungs as well. The pollution on earth is staggering. It's very calm here. I know it's not permanent. We are en route to God knows where.'

I switched on the light, sat up in bed and looked around. Not another sound was heard. I had to be content with that. Now, my head was full of him.

Waking or sleeping, I was waiting for his return. I still had to go to school, help in the garage, and do Christmas shopping.

I called round to his parents. They were quite sprightly. I do believe Andy was actually whistling in his office. We had tea. Eithne was bursting to tell me something.

'Benny, don't think we are crazy, but Christopher spoke to us last night.'

They blushed.

'He visited me as well. None of us is crazy. I was delighted to hear his voice.'

'Us too. Maybe he will visit again over Christmas.'

Eithne got Christopher's painting of the ship at sea.

'I know he was to give it to you for your birthday,

but we felt you should have it now. We also want you to have his copy of To Kill a Mockingbird.'

I had a lump in my throat, but I was pleased.

'I won't look at it 'til my birthday. I've got to honour the deal we made with each other. My birthday is in June.'

'We'll be in the States for Christmas. Andy is lecturing for a semester in Buffalo, New York. We're going early to distract ourselves. You'll visit his grave on Christmas Day, won't you, Benny?'

We were all sad again, but I promised I would.

'Staying here would be heartbreaking for you both.'

'We won't be any better in New York. It will be a distraction. That's all.'

'Are ye putting up a tree?'

'No. How could we come back and see it still up at Easter? But I want you to do something.'

She produced a snowman made of cotton wool.

'He made this in Senior Infants. Will you put it on your tree? He was always comfortable in your house.'

'I will, of course. And we'll have the candle in the window on Christmas night to welcome anyone who needs shelter.'

There was nothing left to say. Eithne hugged me.

Mrs Mc invited Mr O'Brien for Christmas Day. The carol singers stopped outside each of their houses, and the Lions Club filled a hamper for each of them. Cassie was delighted to deliver them.

Our house was awash with Christmas. The tree was a thing of beauty. The crib was in front of the tree. We had holly on the pictures – old-fashioned, sure, but Dad insisted.

Mam went down to Cassie's house to talk to her

mother. The news was not good. Her mam was going to her sister's for Christmas and taking Cassie. She didn't care what the dad did. He could have Christmas on his own, except Cassie wasn't having any of that.

'I'm not going to Aunt Freda's house. She doesn't like me, and her kids are weird. If I stay with Dad, I'll be in my own house at least.'

But the dad was baling as well. He was going to his mother's to lick his wounds.

There was only one thing to be done – Mam had to invite Cassie for Christmas. It wasn't a good idea, but was the least painful option. For Ellen and I, the news was an early Christmas present. Ellen would have Cassie in her bedroom. They could giggle and cuddle to their heart's content. They could discuss boys – especially Howard. Undoubtedly, the attributes of the guys they thought were gorgeous would be on the agenda. They might even discuss me! I admit it, sometimes I listened outside Ellen's door when they were within. Laughter being infectious, and having no company, I yearned for the fun and joy emanating from my twin's room.

It made the loss of Christopher raw all over again. Not that we ever cuddled or giggled in my bed, but we could have laughed ourselves silly about all sorts. After the week I spent sleeping in Ellen's room, it struck me that I had never asked Christopher to come for an overnight stay. I hadn't stayed in his house either. I had been there early morning, long afternoons and until my midnight curfew, but never to sleep.

Usually, we spent Christmas Day on our own. It was a luxury for Dad to close the garage until the New Year. The pumps and the shop would stay open until three p.m. on Christmas Day. All the staff would head for home, anxious to be among their loved ones in the bleak midwinter.

Opening up our home to another, while being the best of Christian behaviour, would be different. I thought about how every family puts its own interpretation on the big day. Some people hang their cards on pieces of string, others place them on a mantle or windowsill. There are fake and natural trees, lots of baubles or few, flashing lights or stable. Every tree in every house is decorated in a personal way.

Christmas was always wonderful in our house. This one would be happy with Cassie among us. But there would be no Christopher. The chance of him sleeping on my floor was nil.

Rules were introduced. There was to be no drinking. Cassie could have a glass of mulled wine with all of us on Christmas night and a glass of wine with her Christmas dinner. Not a drop of vodka would be allowed past the doorstep. Her rucksack would be searched, and she could make other arrangements if she didn't like that.

Ellen and I had to spend a few hours in the shop in the days before Christmas. Cassie helped Ellen as the place was bustling. Mam and Dad were afraid that Cassie might rob some money, so she was warned that the float and the takings had to tally up precisely with the machine. She almost left our house at that stage in disgust, but her options were very limited. It was our house or her Auntie Freda's. She stayed.

I worked an afternoon shift. As Christmas Day would be short, people spent serious money on fuel. I was very busy. I refused to wear a Santa hat, as I had no sense of bonhomie or ho, ho, ho. I did smile at the customers and was able to wish them a happy Christmas.

I got the feeling that Christopher was lounging above the coffee machine. If he was, he had no interest in communication. Perhaps it was a way of supporting me.

It made me wish sincerely for a Christmas night visit.

It was dark by the time I left the shop. I like the town on winter nights. Christmas ones augment the streetlights. Tinsel and baubles glisten from shop windows and homes. I had to smile at a gift I saw in a pharmacy window. The box read 'Good in Bed'. I wondered what it was, and saw it was three different sprays to send you to sleep. Christopher would have enjoyed that, and I would have enjoyed telling him about it.

Howard came over. We played computer games and watched Netflix. I was more comfortable with Howard present. If the girls giggled off to Ellen's room, at least I had company. I told nobody about Christopher in the shop. They would say it was stress or grief. It was all of the above – my feelings were still tumbling like clothes in a washing machine. I had my doubts as well. Did I imagine it? Did I want to hear his voice so badly that I had conjured his spirit? Now, I was waiting for his next manifestation. Once was not enough. Now that I had a link with the other side, surely he could come back to see me at will? I placed his snowman near my own one from Senior Infants. I smiled to notice that mine was almost bereft of cotton wool. Christopher's one showed his early artistic talent

– even the sugar paper eyes were still in situ.

I fell asleep with a warm, fuzzy feeling all around me. I guessed that Christopher was somewhere, but he wasn't in a talking mood. Whispering went on very late in the next room. Ellen was lucky that she had a double bed, so they both could stretch out or curl up and still be comfortable.

Dad put up the crib. St Joseph had had a flat nose since the Christmas when we were four. We'd lost the donkey, but we had a replacement, which was much too small. He may have come from a Monopoly set. The cow was as good as new. The shepherds were few, but the kings were majestic. While Ellen, Cassie and I prepared the table on Christmas Eve, Dad did the crib. The kitchen was full of beautiful smells: the ham boiling, mince pies baking, mulled wine on the hob.

We waited for Dad to rig up the red bulb behind the crib. With the stable lined with brown paper, the light brought shadows around the scene. The Baby Jesus had been washed in Fairy liquid. No one would guess his vest was two thousand years old! The three kings were tucked away behind the stable. We let them in on New Year's Eve. If we waited until January 6th, they would only get a few hours with the child.

On Christmas Eve, Howard called, and we headed for Mass. I couldn't concentrate. Christopher should have been there. We would all have returned to our house for mince pies and a glass of mulled wine. We could have stayed up late and listened to the Carols from King's.

Mam and Dad had piled presents under the tree while we had been away. We did stay up late, and the carols were brilliant. The big light was off, and only the tree lights winked and glowed. It was so cosy, welcoming and quiet. I felt there was a thread linking the five of us in the sharing of the carols. The boy soprano sang, the contralto, bass and the full choir. Their surplices sparked pure white. The lessons were read clearly. Mam stood and found the baby Jesus. She placed him in the crib. We stood around the crib and sang 'Silent Night'. I felt a little hand in mine and I hoped Cassie would have a happy Christmas in our house.

Conscious that we were only allowed one glass of mulled wine, we saved it for midnight, and helped ourselves to mince pies.

Dad gave the toast.

'To absent friends.'

NINE

We left the candle lighting and the hall light on. On Christmas Eve, the youngest family member lights the candle. It is then placed on a windowsill – well away from curtains – to shine all night long. People believed that if anyone travelled without a place to stay, they would see the light in the window and know they were welcome. The Christ Child, Mary and Joseph could find no room at the inn. If they found themselves abroad on this blessed night, they would find shelter and comfort within.

Being the youngest, the task fell to me. Mam took safety seriously, so the big wax candle was housed in a lantern. I placed it on the kitchen window, where it shone through the dark night. I thought it would be a useful signal for a particular soul on this night. He would have placed a candle in his own window. This was Christopher's first Christmas away from home.

The crib bulb was covered with an orange star for the Christmas season. That orange star had been one of our favourite things. There were presents under the tree. I could hear the girls still whispering as I climbed into bed. I didn't know whether I wanted Christopher to arrive or not. I wanted him to be here like Cassie was with Ellen – a real self. I was warm and cosy, but

I was chilly in another way. I thought of the bones in the cemetery and how nature turned all to dust. The giggling from the next room only added to my loneliness.

'Hark the herald angels sing,' emanated from the top of the wardrobe.

'And a happy Christmas to you, too.'

I was wise enough now not to sit up or put on the light.

'You spotted the candle in the window?'

'I saw no candle. Of course, I remember the message. Benny, my friend, I do not need any light to get myself here. The path to you is my prime focus.'

'I'm glad. Were you in the shop earlier today?'

'In the shop?'

'I got a feeling that you were resting above the coffee machine.'

'There's nothing like the smell of real coffee. I loved coffee and croissants. Ah, the tree is a thing of beauty. And of all things, you have my snowman in with your own.'

'Your mam asked me, and I was delighted.'

A sigh escaped from on high.

'You were supposed to be here for the Mass and the carols.'

'And the mince pies and the mulled wine. Indeed, I know.'

'I'm going to the cemetery later.'

'I want you to know that I'm not there.'

'Your bones are. People have always honoured the dead.'

'As they should. This is how it goes. The body is like a deep-sea diver's suit. Essential 'til the moment of death, but useless after. I discarded the body suit and flew away about my own business. I'm still learning the ropes. This place is like an airport. We are all on a stopover, waiting for our flight to be called.'

'It's not getting any easier to accept you being gone. I never thought that you wouldn't be here for Christmas. You were supposed to come to Midnight Mass and then back here for the mulled wine and the mince pies.'

'I wanted you down at mine for Christmas Eve.'

'No matter now.'

'People of fifteen are not supposed to die. Three score and ten are the years allotted as far back as biblical times,' I said.

'You should get in touch with Matt. He's been missing you since he moved. Yes, he has new friends and is well-settled. Phone him and invite him for a few days. You need to get back to playing chess.'

'You need to get back here. Art isn't the same, neither is Woodwork.'

'Get over yourself and your love of the past. Look at the present, and be so grateful that you can still breathe.'

Silence.

I closed my eyes and wished for sleep. I drifted off, and I found a living Christopher in my dream. We were riding our bikes as far as the lake. We knew every turn on the road – up the hill after the grey church, freewheel as far as Kelly's tree, flat along by the new houses, the holy well and on through the quiet woodland to the lapping water of the lake.

The day was hot and sticky. The diving 'board' was a strategically placed boulder. We needed to connect

A Boat for Benny

with the water way out past the clinging weeds. We dived off the rock, shocked by the cold of the reedy water, then laughed, dived again, and shivered.

I woke up shivering as I had kicked off the duvet.

I needed a mug of cocoa. I sipped it and peeped out the kitchen window. Frost had thickened, and even the grass was glistening. I was the only one awake in the house. Not a sliver of anxiety pulled at my head. No thoughts were banging or crashing like bumper cars around my brain. Even Cassie's issues didn't crowd my skull. Perhaps this is peace, the calm, the dark night, a night of hope. Such silence! Not a breath of wind stirred around the house. The stars were glowing. Frost was already visible from rooftops and cars. I hoped Santa wouldn't be delayed en route.

Would that silence remain?

Our house is an easy house. When we moved in, the house seemed to sigh in relief. Though it had a high, pointed roof that reached up above the trees, once we arrived, the house seemed to settle itself and welcome us into its arms. Antique furniture and fine drapes would have suited the proportions, but Mam was not that type.

I thought of Scrooge and the ghosts that visited him. They each had a message. Chris's spirit would always be welcome here. I drifted off to sleep again. I woke at seven-thirty to Dad shaking me.

'Happy Christmas,' he whispered. 'I need you to give me a hand, Benny.'

He put his finger to his lips. I pulled on tracksuit bottoms and a hoodie. We grabbed gloves and scarves. It was a damp, drizzly morning as Dad led the way to the shed.

'This is a surprise for your mother,' he said.

He removed a pile of sacking to reveal the remains of a kitchen dresser. It stood, a black colossus, a gloomy aura emanating from it.

'Your mother has wanted to restore one of these for ages. I've been on the lookout for a long while now.'

'It's covered in black paint, Dad.'

'Bringing it back to the true wood is half the fun.'

We hauled it in. Where plates and cups would sit was easy enough, but the lower half was dead weight and much heavier. We stood the parts in the sitting room far away from the Christmas tree.

'I hope she doesn't think the work is beyond her, Dad.'

'Your mother has a will of iron.'

We stood it up, and he covered it again in the sacking. 'Do not touch' was printed on a card. He tied a purple ribbon on the front.

It struck me then that Dad loved Mam. He had gone to the bother of sourcing the dresser, paid for it, and hid it. He waited until the last moment to secure the surprise because giving her something that would make her happy would make him happy. He was hoping and praying that she would be pleased.

She is a 'make do and mend' kind of woman. She made all the curtains herself and sanded and stained the sitting room floor. Cushions and rugs splash with colour. Our crockery is a mixture of all sorts.

'Just to say, son.'

'Yes, Dad?'

'She will have to go home.'

'I know that. She will.'

'I realise she is in a bad way. Look, we'll enjoy

Christmas Day together. She won't not get drunk here. We'll think of other things tomorrow. Today is Christmas.'

As the oven heated up, the smell of mince pies filled the air. I skipped upstairs to call Christopher about Dad and the dresser.

The shock. Of course, it was the most natural thing to do. He would have laughed at hearing about us puffing and panting while hauling the obstacle indoors.

Then the shivering started. I could feel my heart thumping in my ears. Grief is like that. It hits you when you least expect it. I was doing something lovely with my dad on a day celebrated all over the world, but I wanted to share the smile with only one person. That person was no longer ten minutes away on the other side of town. Though he had been with me a few hours before, I wanted him back now.

Dad called me down for tea. He noticed I was not myself. I told him.

'You'll miss him for years,' he said. 'Not all the time. Life does go on. You'll be getting on with life, and a memory will come flying back that has nothing to do with that day or what you're doing. When our Helen was killed, I was haunted for years by her singing, "How much is that doggy in the window?" She was twenty when she died, but I still heard her child's voice.'

I had nothing to say. The morning moved on. People were busy with dinner and gifts. Though I had planned it, I had no business near that painting. The ship would have to stay at sea for another day, another time. I needed to be in the middle of my family.

Maybe I even needed another aching soul nearby, in Cassie. The difference was her folks were only miles away.

By midday, we were getting ready for dinner. Our presents lay before us in all their glory. Cassie had done well because Ellen had whispered in Mam's ear. We drank the tea and demolished the top layer of the Chocolate Kimberleys. When Howard arrived, he tucked in, savouring the Kimberley and the mince pies.

'We won't eat until about four,' Mam said. 'Ye might like to take a walk to the cemetery.'

I didn't want to see a layer of grass with a small wooden cross, but I would go because I had told his mam that I would. The town was quiet. The last Mass had been said, but the church would remain open for visits to the crib.

There was no room for guff at a grave on Christmas Day. I never meant to cry. After all, he had returned to visit me the previous night and might again.

'I miss you,' I said.

The others hugged me and said I could always talk to them. But they had no clue of the well of grief that felt bottomless.

Every house does Christmas its way. We all know the signs of an Irish Christmas. The turkey order is placed early in December. The pork butcher is asked to reserve a ham. Packets of Christmas cards are bought. The ones for Australia and America have a photo of the town and 'Greetings from Derrybawn' on them. For local greetings, charity cards are favoured. Mam hasn't baked a Christmas Cake for several years. She was the only one who ate it, and as she said, 'All those calories. My stomach is big enough already.'

Dad liked pudding, but Mam had never learned suet puddings. Aunt Rita sent one up from County Clare. Mam made trifle for Ellen and me. We liked it with custard and cream. We wanted a tall tree with lots of fairy lights. We hung baubles old and new. Several of our primary school efforts had pride of place.

At Howard's house, they had loads of decorations outside the house, but Mam wouldn't have that.

'It's what's on the inside that counts.'

We ate when it was dark outside. We liked to have candles on the table, and the crystal glassware got its annual outing. The plates were part of a wedding present. Our table didn't look like this any other day of the year. The white linen cloth had been ironed perfectly. The settings of red charger plates, Newgrange cutlery, Waterford glass and napkins were lovely. The sideboard held the trifle bowl, the pudding, the tin of Afternoon Tea biscuits and boxes of Roses, Quality Street and Celebrations.

Oh, the taste of the turkey, the smell of cloves in the ham, the roast potatoes, stuffing and gravy! The cook was complimented. Though we were full, we called for the trifle, and Dad had his slice of pudding. Having no better toast for a Christmas dinner than Dickens, we raised our glasses, saying, 'God bless us, everyone.'

It was a fine Christmas. My mother was impressed with the dresser – or the dresser bits. She is the kind of woman who can see possibilities where others would be stumped. There was wool everywhere! There were signs of her knitting – cotton bags on the backs of kitchen chairs or tucked into a corner of the couch.

We moved into the sitting room to the big TV. It wasn't so much that we wanted to watch anything, but that the couches were big and soft, as were we after our feast.

We watched Miracle on 34th Street. At the relevant moment, we all said, 'I believe'. We followed that with It's a Wonderful Life. It's amazing how many Christmas sweets you can eat, even with a full stomach. I took all the Bounties out of the tin, and Cassie stole the Galaxies. Mam and Dad shared the Roses, and Ellen was well into the Quality Street.

We put the candle in the window again, in case Christopher or any other souls were passing by.

By New Year's Eve, there was still no sign of either of Cassie's parents. Their shop was due to reopen on the second of January. Having finished Christmas, Cassie was anxious to return to her bedroom, clothes, and privacy. She wanted to stretch out in her bed, hug a pillow, and maybe cry into it in peace. We walked down to the crib.

'I don't know why I'm so down. Your problem is so much bigger than mine. Christopher is never coming back.'

'Well, I don't think it's a competition, Cassie. We're both sad. That's the fact.'

'Whatever happens with my folks, they're still here. Even if they hate each other's guts, they're still breathing.'

I had nothing to reply. We arrived at her house.

'We are always in your house. We never go to Howard's, and we never come here.'

'You come to see Ellen. Howard comes to see me,

supposedly. We all know he is mad about Ellen. I'm just there because I live there.'

We sat in the kitchen, and she made tea. The place was very tidy, and the work surfaces were clear. The milk was almost off, but I said nothing.

'I like you,' she said.

'I like you too.'

'You and Christopher were always together. I couldn't get a look in.'

'I was admiring you from a distance.'

'Until I vomited all over your shoes and jeans, and you brought me home.'

I said nothing.

'And Christopher was killed.'

I drank the chalky tea.

'If I…'

'You can "if" forever, Cassie. It changes nothing. You were sick. I know it was from vodka. Someone had to make sure you got home. Christopher knew I liked you for ages. He knew what I needed to do that night.'

'I will always feel responsible, Benny, I will. What was happening here had scrambled my brains, and the vodka took the pain away. I hadn't even told Ellen the full story.'

'At home, they're all watching me – afraid I'll crack up. How can I explain my grief to anyone? I miss him so much. I never thought I would have to spend a Christmas without him.'

She started to cry.

'Look around this place,' she said. 'Not a candle, a tree, a decoration. Not a present in sight or a half-empty tin of Roses. So full of themselves and their issues. Would you abandon your child at Christmas, Benny?'

'Let's go, Cassie. Being here is doing you no good.'

'Come and see my room,' she said.

At this point, my Adam's apple was like a ball in my throat.

It was a square room at the back of the house. The window looked out at trees. Under the window, there was an old green leather chair.

'That's my reading spot,' she said.

Around the walls were shelves and shelves of books. Several of the titles were stacked on my shelves at home. Cassie's desk was an old oak table. On the wall behind were sketches of animals and plants, handwritten poems and feathers. Her bed was covered with a blanket of many colours.

'I've got a few of these books at home.'

'We need to discuss reading at some stage. Do you like Steinbeck?'

'I have The Red Pony. I did enjoy it. You've To Kill a Mockingbird and The Catcher in the Rye. I've read those as well.'

I noticed a small collection of poetry books.

'You read poetry?'

'Don't you?'

'Only for the exam.'

'You're missing so much.'

'Christopher was the poetry lover.'

'I wish I had known that.'

'He was crazy about sonnets.'

'I like them myself.'

I flicked through one of the books.

'So, who are The Mersey Sound?'

A Boat for Benny

'Going back a long way there. There was a big poetry movement in the sixties. The Mersey Sound came out of Liverpool around the time of The Beatles.'

'And Mary Oliver?'

'An American poet, not long dead. One of my favourites of hers is "Wild Geese".'

'Of course I know who Seamus Heaney is. Aren't we doing "Follower" for the exam?'

'We'll make a poetry lover out of you yet, Benny Cullen.'

The layout of her room was good. There were no clothes on the floor. She had a huge wardrobe. Underneath, her shoes were neatly lined up.

'I could live in a room like this,' I said.

'Your own room is cool. I noticed the pictures of Christopher.'

'They're all I have left to remind me of him.'

'You have loads of memories, Benny. The best of memories.'

'I want the guy himself, Cassie – the real flesh and blood Chris.'

She let it be. She was wise enough to realise that there were no words to help me.

'I love it here,' she said. 'I feel far from the town when I see my trees. I can be a world away in my reading corner. When I'm at the table, I imagine I'm writing some great tome which may change the world.'

'And that cap? Isn't that a copy of the one Jo March wore in Little Women?'

'Lie down,' she said. 'I'll read you something.'

'Of your own?'

'No, idiot.'

I lay down on the blanket, but she pulled it and put it over me. She climbed in. In a quiet voice, she read Robert Frost's 'Acquainted with the Night'.

I couldn't say anything. I reached for Cassie's hand under the cover, and she held mine. We fell asleep. She grabbed a few books and a notebook an hour later, and we headed back to ours.

'I went down to check out the house, and Benny came with me,' she said, heading upstairs with the stuff she had brought.

'Everything okay?' my mam asked.

'Yep,' Cassie said, 'apart from the fact that the milk's gone off.'

'Well, your mam rang. She will be back tomorrow. You can get milk and bread in our shop early in the morning. We'll be closed from midday.'

New Year's Eve had come, but we would not be heading out. There was no teenage disco, or anywhere else to go. It was looking fairly grim. Mam announced that Howard would be coming over. We could have a few cans and watch whatever we liked. They were heading to the pub but would return to ring in the New Year.

The girls got dressed up, even though they were going nowhere. Howard arrived in his usual gear, the sleeveless denim jacket looking a bit grubby. I had been caught on the hop. Tracksuit bottoms and a hoodie did nothing for my appearance. I told myself I was at home in my own house, I was in good humour and all would be well.

It took the girls ages to get downstairs. They both looked lovely, though I doubted the eyelashes were theirs. Ellen was wearing a skirt so short it looked like a belt. Cassie had the tightest leggings I had ever seen. Their tops hugged their figures. They looked like models. Howard and I were struck dumb. This was the first time we had seen them made up like that at home. Was it for us or themselves? We had no idea.

'You dressed up to watch TV?' Howard said, blinking.

Ellen told Howard to follow her into the kitchen.

Cassie said, 'This is how I like to dress up, Benny.'

'Great. Yes. I'm just surprised.'

'You don't seem that impressed.'

'You look amazing. But I was impressed when you read to me yesterday. I think you're beautiful with your own face.'

'I don't like tracksuit bottoms on anyone,' she said.

'I'm at home and chilling out. I'm not getting dressed up. Take me or leave me. I don't like artificial eyelashes.'

There were raised voices in the kitchen. Cassie sat down, and I hovered.

'Sit beside me anyway,' she said.

I sat down. She smelled lovely. Really, from the neck down, she was the Cassie I fancied and loved, but the muck on her face was too much for me. The other two soon appeared. Ellen's eye makeup was running down her face, and her lipstick was smudged. She and Cassie headed back upstairs.

'What's going on?' Howard whispered.

'I have no idea. Cassie has false eyelashes.'

'Maybe there is something wrong with the two of us, Benny. I hate all that makeup.'

'I know, but they like it. I don't want to make them

miserable tonight.'

We sneaked up to my room. I put on chinos and a clean shirt. Howard kept his jeans but agreed to wear an open navy t-shirt and my denim shirt. We washed our faces, threw on some deodorant and a drop of aftershave, and took our seats.

The girls came down the stairs, having repaired their faces. Their makeup had been newly applied, but the eyelashes were the same as before. They looked at us, and all four of us laughed.

'Let's open the beer, the last box of Celebrations and watch The Muppet Christmas Carol.'

Howard and Ellen were used to fitting into the big armchair. Cassie and I took the two-seater. We ate, drank and laughed. There were cosy and private moments, but we kept our clothes on.

When Mam and Dad returned, we were ready to welcome the New Year. Only Christopher was missing – but that was a serious loss.

A Boat for Benny

TEN

Cassie left early on New Year's Day. She wanted to turn on the heat, light the fire, and buy a few basics. I spent the first few hours in the shop, and Ellen would take over at ten.

'Come down to mine for coffee when you finish,' Cassie said.

'I will so,' I said. 'You might read me something else.'

'Wait and see,' she winked, and my heart sang.

I was excited. I was invited down on my own. I would not be part of the scenery. I would be the guest. I hoped we would have coffee in her room and that I could sit on the leather chair. I knew I wanted to.

Her parents were home. I hesitated, but I wanted to see Cassie. She opened the door, stepped out and put her arms around me.

'You're coming in. You must.'

'Happy New Year,' I said to all present.

'Hello, Benny. Will you have tea?' her mam asked.

'We're having coffee in my room,' Cassie replied.

I followed her upstairs. If those in the kitchen didn't like how things were going, they had enough sense to keep quiet. She pulled her study chair over to the window. She gave me the leather chair. She pulled a tin of Chocolate Kimberleys from her sock drawer.

'Take off your boots,' she said. 'You can put your feet on the radiator and enjoy the view.'

There we were, two innocents abroad – tranquil, serene and easy. This was the first time I had been invited to take off my boots and reveal my thick socks in a girl's presence. She was a brave woman.

'I don't know what's going to happen here,' she said. 'Granny Downey told Dad to sort out marriage counselling. Aunt Freda told Mam to act her age, sort it out or divorce him. Watch this space.'

'I brought something to read,' I said.

'That was brave of you. How do you know what I like?'

I read a piece at the end of To Kill a Mockingbird. It's where Boo Radley comes out of the shadows and takes Scout's hand. She brings him in to see Jem in bed. Cassie had tears in her eyes. She squished into the leather chair beside me, and squeezed my hand.

'It would be lovely to nap like yesterday, but we won't, given the circumstances. I'll come up to yours in the afternoon to collect my stuff. I'll see you then. I might bring some poetry because you need plenty of exposure. Will I bring The Mersey Sound book?'

'Do. Dad is well into The Beatles, so why not?'

Later on, I waited and waited. I asked Ellen if Cassie had sent any messages. In the evening, her mam arrived.

'Cassie's in the hospital. She has an acute appendicitis. The pain started at lunchtime. It was vicious. She is having an operation now. I'll grab some stuff she had left here.'

A Boat for Benny

I had enough sense to grab Mockingbird and give it to her.

'Cassie will understand,' I said.

I went to my room to hide because I was shivering all over, and my stomach was sick. I tried to tell myself that this was a common occurrence. Even though it required an operation, the surgeons would do their job. She would be home in a few days. There would be tiny stitches, and she would be as good as new. Maybe now her folks would start behaving like adults. And I would get a chance to sit in the leather chair again.

Cassie was in the local hospital, nothing like the high-tech place where Christopher had died. There were no machines, and a drip line fed antibiotics into her. I was glad to see that she was awake.

'I got an awful fright, Cassie.'

'I told myself he'll think it is the big hospital. He'll be thinking of Christopher. That's why I sent Mam to your house.'

'How do you feel now?'

'The awful pain is gone. But Benny, I'm sore all over. I want to sleep.'

Before my eyes, she drifted off. I sat for a little while, just listening to her breathe, knowing that when she woke up, she would feel better. But much more important was knowing she would wake up and I would see her again. So much of my life experience now refers back to Christopher's accident and death. I never want to enter that hospital again, because of the shock, panic and grief. It was good to see Cassie with her eyes open. I knew she was conscious, and her own heart was doing its job. She drifted off to sleep so easily, I felt safe to leave her on her own. No monitors or alarms would beep.

We took it easy for the days before our return to school. The kings were returned to the attic, and were followed by all the other Christmas stuff. Hetty and I called to Mrs Mc and Mr O, and stashed away their Christmas stuff, too.

'We'll expect the same service next December,' she said. 'We want the two of you back.'

'You gave me back the Christmas spirit,' Mr O said.

Hetty smiled. 'It was there all the time. It just needed a gentle nudge.'

'Same again for me too,' he said.

I knew that looking ahead was a bad idea. So many things can trip you up. I was only away from Christopher for about two hours, and he died. He had invited me to a Lucien Freud exhibition at the IMMA just after Christmas. It would have been a first for me.

Even though Cassie didn't do Art as an exam subject, I noticed how well she could draw. I hadn't mentioned the sketches on her wall, but I noticed them. Maybe she would come to the IMMA.

ELEVEN

Exam papers marked our return to school. We had booklets of questions from previous years. We answered them in school and at home. Specific topics were being kept for after the mocks, but anything covered from the beginning of Second Year could turn up. I remember Christopher talking to me about the Renaissance. We looked at Michelangelo's work in Florence and Leonardo's there and elsewhere.

'Someday, we'll go to Florence and see the real thing. I want to see the "David" so much.'

'You're an artist in your soul,' I said.

'For a history buff like you, Benny, it will be great. The place where the Medici rose to power and the interactions between the Papal States and the other regions in Italy.'

Silly old me. At the time, I had looked up the Ryanair flights. I knew you flew into Pisa and got the bus to Florence from the airport. If I ever got to Tuscany, it would not be with Christopher. If I managed to get to Enniscorthy Castle, he wouldn't be there to explain the significance of Eileen Gray's work either. Imagine a woman born and raised a few miles from here whose designs for houses, chairs and tables are admired worldwide. Two heads are always better than one. I would have the historical context for the works of art we would discover, and Christopher would plan the itinerary. I would book the flights, accommodation and tours. We had reckoned that we had years and years of art breaks ahead of us. Architecture would have to be included, and we'd travel by train because we both liked them. We had made a bucket list a mile long, and when we were men of the world, making money, we would indulge our interests in Art and History.

'We don't have to worry about Paris,' Chris had said. 'We'll be going there on the Transition Year trip.'

'Well, Amsterdam for sure. The Rijksmuseum and Vincent.'

'Good call.'

'Rome for the antiquities.'

'Our already-beloved Florence.'

I shook myself and tried to get back to the task at hand: studying. But then I heard a sound.

'Come down from the clouds and get back to work.'

'What about a gentle greeting to ease a guy's mind?'

'Do you know what you are, Ben, old son?'

'I'm waiting.'

'A procrastinator and a ditherer.'

'I'm working away here. I am.'

'In fairness, you're doing the history of art, the types of wood joints, English poetry, the play and nothing else.'

'Well, I have plenty of time to do the rest.'

'Benny, come on. You're staying in your comfort zone.'

'I know, and you know why, don't you?'

'Because that's where you find traces of me.'

'It's my way of staying connected to how things were.'

We both stayed quiet for a few minutes. I enjoyed knowing he was nearby without speaking.

'People really have it made when they only need one name.'

'Aha, a light has come on.'

'Geniuses are known by one name. Michelangelo is sufficient, and so is Leonardo. Everyone knows Elvis, Prince, Messi and Galileo.'

'A good point, but the rest of us need two – even on a tombstone.'

I didn't appreciate being swung back to reality, and that was a bit below the belt.

'The algebra will need some work.'

'I know, but Ellen says my geometry and arithmetic will get me the honour.'

'Well, you must know the algebraic equations by heart.'

'I'll have them remembered for when I need them.'

'What's new with you?'

'I'm bored stiff. I've read all the books and people change all the time. I settle with a group, and they are moved on while a new group arrives. I'd say I'm due to ship out soon.'

I panicked when he said this. However odd our communication was, I had become used to it and accepted it – but now feared it would end.

'I'm not ready to survive without you yet.'

'I wasn't ready to go. I want to come back. I want to wake up, discover it was all a bad dream, climb back into my black chinos and leather coat and meet you for coffee, a Coke or even a 99.'

I wanted to cry, howl even. No one returns from the dead and climbs back into their old life. Sometimes, I would ask myself if my brain was conjuring him up like a crutch for me to lean on. Was I inventing his presence to soothe myself and make the pain ease off? Was it Benny One and Benny Two in the conversation?

'There could be a bit of confusion these days with Leonardo. That actor is very well known.'

I was about to reply but realised he had already left. Spirits don't always say goodbye.

It was time for me to get my act together. There were six other subjects apart from Art. I expected to reach an A in honours English, since it was my favourite subject. Apart from coursework, I knew I could write a good essay. But there is no place for arrogance before you're hit with the real papers. People talked about topics that would 'turn up again' because they were always turning up, but if you hadn't studied the course to date, an A or a high B was beyond your reach.

Sometimes Ellen studied with me. She was a whizz at Maths. She had little patience with me because I was poor at algebra.

The four of us decided we would need a break on Friday nights. We headed home directly after school, changed out of our uniforms and rejoiced that we were free for the next twenty-four hours. The chip dinner arrived. Everyone tucked in, and sometimes we headed for the cinema.

Privacy is a rare event in any teenager's house. I knew I could sit close to Cassie at the cinema. I could even kiss her, perhaps with my tongue. I could try other moves, too, but every girl had her limit – and I'd attempt to push it at my peril.

The mocks were completed in ten days in February. Easter was late, so we had class again for six weeks before the break. We were working hard, getting to grips with new stuff. We wondered if our brains could take much more.

I liked going to Cassie's house. Her bedroom was really a place of relaxation. Oh, sitting in that leather chair with a book in my hand, I could sail many rivers. I mentioned the visit to the Museum of Modern Art. We could change the dates on the tickets.

'Study is about as much as I can handle now, Benny. Sorry.'

'It's on for all of this year. There's no rush.'

Though it was hardly approved of, I sometimes studied in Cassie's house. I sat in the leather chair and answered questions on Goodnight Mister Tom. I had to study the characters and make decisions about them. I could take whatever approach I wanted, but I would need to back up my position with examples from the text. Cassie worked on Higher Maths problems at her desk.

We hardly got more than an hour before her mam shouted up, 'Come on, Benny, time to go.'

We weren't having a session in her bedroom, in broad daylight with her mother downstairs, and with work piling up like dirty clothes!

The same thing happened in our house when Cassie and Ellen were working on Maths or Business Studies. Howard came to our house as well, so I would then be on my own as the three Maths-heads worked in their rarified atmosphere.

Ellen wouldn't go to Howard's place even for coffee, never mind co-ordinating geometry.

TWELVE

Out of the blue, one of the great wonders of the world was realised. The Year Head decided we needed a break, so we were brought to visit the West for St Patrick's weekend. We travelled down on one of Roche's Coaches, and four staff members came with us. We stayed in the hostel in Leenane. There were dorms with bunks, single-sex only.

Of course, there were couples on the trip who were closely observed by the staff. The people who liked alcohol were also on their radar, as well as those who smoked. It was a given that one staff member would be the bane of every trip. The other three usually saw the big picture, but the fourth would be difficult. We had been warned.

Mr Matthews was going through a divorce. He had been like a demon for the past several months. He seemed to take his anger towards his wife out on the girls. They were laughing too loudly. They were painting their toenails, and he didn't like the cloying smell. Someone had been smoking dope. He could smell it, but couldn't find the culprit. We understood his life was falling apart, but that wasn't our fault.

There was a rota for cooking. We arrived late on

A Boat for Benny

Thursday, so it was pizza and salad. We had a bit of a sing-song in the common room before heading for bed. I didn't sleep well. At home, my room was dark and had no shadows. Here, there were outside lights. People were snuffling and coughing. For me, sleep is about peace, quietness and the dark. All the better if I have read a calming few pages of a decent novel. If Christopher visited, my excitement would keep me awake afterwards. I would take a visit from Christopher over a sleep, anytime.

I scrunched up in the bed, wrapped the duvet as tightly as possible, and waited. I could hear snuffling, coughing and loud breathing. I wanted to turn them all down. The duvet was too warm. I stuck my feet out, thumped the pillow and tried to settle again. I must have drifted off eventually.

Mr Matthews had everyone up by seven-thirty. There was no mercy for people who found it hard to sleep. My eyes felt gritty, and my head was heavy. Several others were in the same state as me. The breakfast crew hadn't expected to be up before nine. We were silent but belligerent. Miss Clancy didn't appear 'til half nine. She and Mr Matthews had words. No matter what time he roused us, she told him she would not be available before ten any morning. We secretly cheered Miss Clancy. They were giving up a long weekend in their holidays to supervise us, and we were grateful.

It was cold but calm, and it'd be a good day for canoeing. The fjord faced west. The sun was behind us as we pulled the canoe to the edge and climbed in. Woollen caps, gloves and scarves were the order of the day. The trainers were clear about safety and water wisdom. As we began there was noise, shouts and laughing. When the canoes moved away from each other, quietness descended. A pale blue sky made the sea blue. The surface of the water was like glass.

When we got into our rhythm, the only sounds were of our paddles pulling through the water, lipping it as they dipped easily and rhythmically, and leaving V-shaped lines behind us. Cassie came in the canoe with me. We said little. The canoe and the two of us worked as one. I thought of how peaceful and healing a few days away could be for us. I remembered Kerry and my snorkelling adventure with Christopher. I had Cassie with me now. For all I knew, Christopher was swimming along beside us. We had never gone snorkelling together, which was such a shame. Connecting with a person under the surface is a special event. Even giving the 'thumbs up' underwater is powerful.

And I did. Though I canoed along with Cassie, I wished there was someone else with me. I wished for Christopher to be alive, strong and here and to do something with him once more. He would have found pictures in the clouds. I would have regaled him with the fact that a fjord is a drowned valley and deeper in the middle than out at sea.

The long, narrow shore of the fjord rose on either side. Conifers marched up the hill on our right. To our left, native deciduous trees were magnificent. We always think of Norway for fjords, but Killary Harbour here in our own country is a perfect example of one.

We heard the whistle, which was our signal to return to the shore.

A Boat for Benny

'I loved that,' Cassie said.

'Me too.'

'The water is so soothing. It takes a lot of tension away.'

'What's on your mind?'

'Ah, same old, same old,' she said. 'They were civil when I was ill, but they're like two elephants now, taking up too much space and not a kind word between them.'

We ate our sandwiches and drank our milk. We had a hike along the south shore in the afternoon. We climbed by the summit and walked back by the beach and woods. There were challenges along the way – negotiating a rope bridge, wading through shallows, and jumping over streams. It was good fun. By the time we reached the hostel, we were weary and famished. It was the best bolognese I had ever tasted! There was so much spaghetti I filled my plate twice. The cooks got a rousing cheer from all of us.

That night, there was chat in the common room. The day's exertions meant that some people headed to bed quite early. We stretched out on a long couch and recounted our days.

'I'd say Christopher would have loved today,' Ellen said.

'He was a good swimmer,' Howard chimed in.

'I still miss him every day. I have a cold feeling in my stomach when I think of him dead.'

'They were bound together like you and me, Ellen, that close,' Cassie said.

We walked to the dorms in silence. It wasn't just me. Howard and the girls missed him, too. I didn't have a monopoly on sadness.

I was so tired that the snuffles or coughs did not affect me. I closed my eyes and thought about the canoe sliding through the water. I could see the cliffs and the other canoes and hear the water ripple as we moved. Oh, blessed sleep to heal the aching heart.

A big adventure had been planned for Saturday. We would leave, head up the Westport Road, enjoy Clew Bay, and climb Croagh Patrick. Miss Clancy announced that we would leave at ten. Mr Matthews said nothing. Mrs O'Driscoll warned that she would do a late-night check of the dorms. Mr McCullough was away in his own world, probably solving Maths problems in his head.

Saturday's plans were scuppered. We woke to a white world. Roche's Coach was going nowhere.

'It's on the itinerary,' Mr Matthews said.

'It could be on the television for all I care,' said the driver. 'I have to take the safety of all of you, plus the vehicle, into account.'

The snow was everywhere down the West Coast. The snow on the beach was a wonderment. Walls, sand and rocks were white. The water was a deep grey, reflecting the ominous clouds above. Watching snow fall on the sea and melt was so unusual. We threw snowballs into the sea. They hardly fizzed. We left prints in the sand, The thaw would come late afternoon, too late for our trip. Mr Matthews was overwhelmed, and I felt sorry for him. What would anyone do with thirty-two students stuck in a winter wonderland without plans or a road to get out?

We had our breakfast – boiled eggs and toast – and we waited. The trainers from the activity centre

A Boat for Benny

arrived with news. We were pretty much cut off. The thaw would set in early enough, but there would be no travel that day.

There was no breeze. Mother Nature was quiet, and the snow was soundless. We asked if we could go canoeing again, as safety wouldn't be an issue since it was so calm.

'No way,' said the head trainer.

Mrs O'Driscoll had no time for moaning and groaning. She organised a snowman-building competition. After that, we had a snowball fight and made snow angels. We weren't fifteen and sixteen anymore. We were ten years old on a day off from school. You forget about people laughing at you when you are fully involved in an activity. Snowballs hit people, we fell in the snow, shivered and had blue fingers from the cold. But our hearts were warm!

And then Mr Matthews found a pile of cardboard boxes in a shed. We flattened them out and headed for a hill. We held on and slid down on them. Some people went head first. As soon as the cardboard was soaked, we picked another piece and off we went again. Howard and Ellen slid down together. Cassie did her own thing, as did I. I thought of Christopher. He would have sat in front, and I would have held on for dear life. As it was, I had to guide it myself, but I managed.

The trainers hung around but could offer us no activity. We were frozen and wet after our mad adventures. They had a Land Rover and brought us milk, drinking chocolate and biscuits. We headed into the common room. The fire was lit, and we all warmed up. The mantle was covered in a line of wet socks, gloves and caps. Steam rose and drips fell onto the hearth. We needed them dry for the morning. The smell of wet wool isn't pleasant.

There was still much of the day left, if not the light. Never were bangers and mash so welcome. Our insides warmed up, and even our toes were cosy in our clean socks.

Mr McCullough was never famous for his after-school interaction with students, but the snow seemed to have had an effect on him – he appeared to have entered a new reality.

After dinner, he said we should pull all the couches and chairs close to the fire. We turned out the big light. The glow and flames from the fire added a whole new dimension. Shadows appeared in corners. Our own shadows appeared like giants on the ceiling and the floor.

He started to tell ghost stories. We all remembered ghost stories from childhood, but they bore no resemblance to Mr McCullough's tales. Many of his ended with no resolution, but people were petrified. There were fairies and the Puca and the Banshee. Sometimes, a bodiless hand appeared, and someone might be lost in a field and never find an exit. It was exciting and fearful, heart-stopping and tantalising. He created an excellent atmosphere and used his voice so well that we were scared stiff.

'I don't know if any of you have heard of the power of May Eve. So many stories are set in wintertime, the short days adding to the darkness and the threat. On May Eve, the light lasts until late. The sun might not set until half-past nine. Not the time you would expect dark deeds to take place.

A Boat for Benny

'On May Eve, the farmers do the "four corners". They walk the whole farm, stopping in each of the four directions. They take out their rosary beads and pray that the land be free from harm for the next year. They continue the walk until sunrise. They sprinkle holy water as well, the better to protect the land.'

Some wit shouted, 'What if they are Protestants?

A deathly silence showed him he was out of order.

'They're doing so to prevent a "piseog" being put on the farm. A piseog is a curse. If that curse is cast on May Eve between midnight and first light, it's believed to be very powerful. Some piseogs were cast using objects that once were alive. A neighbour might throw an egg, a piece of old meat, or even a raven carcass on the farmer's ground to make the piseog stronger. The wish would be for bad luck for the farmer – that his cows wouldn't milk or that the hens would not lay.

'Of course, the lighter side was lighting fires at sunset to celebrate Bealtaine – which means "bright fire". People danced around the maypole to herald the arrival of summer. But don't be fooled – dark deeds were done even on bright nights.'

By bedtime, Mr McCullough had achieved hero status. The thaw had started in the afternoon. We expected to be free to travel home on Sunday. We would eat and leave.

To give the driver his due, he stopped in Athlone on the way home. We were given an hour to spend there, and Cassie and I had great fish and chips and beautiful coffee. She was a good companion. She didn't sweat the small stuff. Her nails were their natural colour.

When I remember that weekend, my sense is of being fully alive. I was myself and felt part of the crowd. Cassie added to my enjoyment of it all. As a group, we bonded over those few days. I was part of a group of my peers. I felt accepted. We thanked Mrs O'Driscoll for the snow fun and Mr McCullough for the ghost stories. Mr Matthews was saluted for persuading the driver to give us time in Athlone. Miss Clancy had done little apart from staying in bed late. Still, that was appreciated, too.

And yet, that night in bed in my own room – where I felt most comfortable – I thought of phoning Christopher. I must have been half asleep because I couldn't understand why he hadn't been away with me. A little sign would have done me good. I recalled that he never spoke to me when others were nearby. I would need to remember that for the future, and keep it to myself. There was nothing to be gained by sharing that thought with others.

I didn't dwell on the piseogs, and yet I believed in bad luck. If Cassie hadn't vomited on me, I wouldn't have had to bring her home. If I had been walking home with Christopher, we wouldn't have been at the fatal spot on the road where he was killed. A split second can change everything.

I had been talking to myself, but now there was another presence.

'You'll have to stop Benny. You'll make yourself sick.'

'But it's true. If…'

'I heard all of those tales as well. I had to keep quiet, but I noticed how enthralled you were.'

'He spun a web, and I was caught fair and square.'

'Do you believe that a curse could make a cow dry?'

'No, but the atmosphere was great: the firelight, the shadows, the dark and his haunting voice.'

'Don't forget your beloved Cassie by your side.'

'Beloved is a bit strong. I'm not sure if we're really an item.'

'Trust me, my brother. That is an item.'

'You're embarrassing me.'

'If I could have had the chance of finding someone…'

He left. Usually, I was the one who vocalised my needs and my wishes. Now, Chris was telling me that he knew what his future didn't hold.

I had thought the loss was all on my side. Now, I knew that he still wanted to be alive. Whatever wit or light-heartedness he usually showed was masked today by his sheer wish to grow up alongside me. Not knowing where we would live or work as adults, or where we would settle, we would still have never been more than a phone call away.

THIRTEEN

Mam said it was only the Junior Cert, and not to worry. Dad agreed with her. I still wanted to do well. I needed reassurance that I had understood the topics and could give acceptable answers. The answers were multiple-choice for some subjects, but you had to make the right choice.

Ellen had a huge capacity for studying. She spent hours in her room perfecting everything. Though Howard had sailed through school since we were in Infants, he studied as if his life depended on it. I wondered if they were challenging each other. Did each of them want to get better grades than the other?

I wanted to get the best result I could. Cassie was focussed on Maths, History and English. She loved all of those and neglected her other subjects. Sometimes, my mind wandered. I would find myself looking at the walls, floor and pictures in my room, and only came back to reality when Mam shouted up the stairs, 'I hope the two of you are working and not taking a rest.'

I could look at the photos on the walls of my room and she would never know. Sometimes, I made simple sketches of two boys climbing, swimming or snorkelling. I could squeeze my eyes closed and call

A Boat for Benny

Christopher in a whisper, but he never replied on cue. He had to instigate our connection. I waited and was grateful for any contact at all.

The mock results arrived. I came out with a B in English and History. The rest of my grades were C, apart from Art, where I had only scraped a D. I was very disappointed. I knew that my monochrome mark had brought me down. Miss Murphy had to forward the results of our school-based assignments. There was no time for fuss. I had to study again.

I would talk to Cassie to get her idea of what Art was about. She would be coming at it from a fresh angle. She drew just for enjoyment. Her ideas might help with my essay. Of course, I knew Christopher was the man to have on my shoulder. He could whisper hints into my inner ear. He might even be able to give me correct answers. Wishful thinking. If he were still alive, he wouldn't believe in cheating. When I think of it, I would hate to be caught cheating in front of him.

April and May were just a blur. The non-exam classes left at the end of May with whoops and shouts. The first of June loomed. There were no manifestations, aural or otherwise. Christopher would not arrive with words of faith, hope or charity. He would come when he wanted to or was able. He was not available at my beck and call. I was the needy one. He had been content in his life, his family and his friends. His best friend meant a lot to him. He never wanted to die. To do my best, I had to live day by day.

I got into exam mode. Religiously, I gave time to each subject and took ages with algebra.

Let x equal 10 and y equal 3. What is the value of $x+y-9$?

I couldn't see the point of these letters, but there was logic behind it. It was a two-step problem.

$x+y=10+3$

$x+y=13$

$x+y-9=13-9=4$

Answer=4

I heard a voice.

'Algebra is not your best topic.'

'Never was, but I've given it my best.'

'You got on well in the West.'

I kept quiet for a few minutes.

'I did. It was great fun, but…'

'I saw it all. It was brilliant fun.'

'I wanted you to slide down the hill with me. I wanted to throw snowballs at you. Were you anywhere near the canoes?'

'I saw the divine Cassie and stayed away.'

'Cassie is not you. No one will ever fit the place you had in my life.'

'Benny, I know that. You had carved out a special spot in my heart.'

'We talked about the ghost stories already.'

'Did we?'

'Yes! That night was great. I wished you were in the dormitory with all the other guys. We could have told our own ghost stories and terrified each other.'

'I've terrified enough people, leaving the world so early and without warning.'

'The exams are in a few days. Will you stay nearby when I take the English, Art and Woodwork papers?'

'Are you seriously asking for my help to cheat?'

'You know I'm not. The papers might be fine, but I'd like to know you were near for support.'

A Boat for Benny

If other things were to be said, this was not the night. The truth can be so powerful that it shocks the speaker and the listener. We let it be.

And yet, I went over the conversation in my head. He had not forgotten anything up to now. What if I was conjuring him out of my own head? Was he gone forever, and I was playing both parts in the conversation?

I knew my geometry theorems by heart, and my Irish irregular verbs were on the tip of my tongue. I could not be caught out on woodworking tools or the ages of a river.

Some days, we had two papers. I did my best, and multiple-choice answers helped a great deal. My confidence built up with the History and Geography papers. I answered several questions about the Renaissance. But the Art paper was a challenge for me. The boy came into my mind. He should have been there a few seats away from me, writing as fast as he could. The essay was on the topic of masks. I had a wobble, and I thought I would start to cry. The ache to see him was a fresh wound in my heart.

I thought of his costume. I remembered the details of the mask, the headdress and the colour green. I had been Gandalf. Dad had sourced the staff for me in the hardware shop. I wrote from my heart. I tuned in to the prep classes and the history of the Venetian Mardi Gras carnival. Like a diver on the high board, I soared through the air before gliding to hit the target. It was all myself, all my own work.

I had no time for memories when it came to the English paper.

'The evil that men do lives after them / The good

is oft interred with their bones.' Comment on how Julius Caesar's legacy proves or disproves the above.

Whichever side I took was acceptable, as long I had quotations from the text to back them up.

The poetry choice was a no-brainer: 'Stopping by Woods on a Snowy Evening' by Robert Frost. I left the essay until last. I could let my imagination soar. I was torn between the subjects of 'Destiny' and 'My Life'.

'Destiny' was the safer option. 'My Life' would have exposed my sadness and my grief. Destiny is unknown. It lies in the future. Yet, an episode in the past had already changed my fate, my destiny. I had to pinch myself. This was an exam. I could waffle on. I would use imagery: clouds blown by the wind, a toy boat that sails out of a stream, a winning lottery ticket thrown into the fire.

I would not mention the boy who had been killed by a drunk driver, or how his destiny had been shattered one October night.

FOURTEEN

During this time, it seemed as if Cassie's parents had called a truce. I felt that they were playing at being parents. They managed to avoid having any physical contact – even a hand brushing off a hand. The ever-present politeness was stultifying.

We escaped to Cassie's room, but it wouldn't be long before I'd hear, 'You'll have to leave soon, Benny. Cassie has to study.'

The same thing happened if Cassie was in our house. Christopher thought it was a fair comment. He voiced his opinion.

'Love is all very well, my boy, but it doesn't get good exam grades. Summer lies ahead. Think of all the time ye can spend together from mid-June,' he whispered.

'I can't wait, loads of free time and no homework – sleeping late, going for coffee, walking up the Furies and getting a bit physical.'

'Don't overwhelm her, Benny. She's had enough to deal with.'

'This is the summer I've been waiting for. I've time, energy, money and enthusiasm. I have needs.'

'Cassie is vulnerable and has been for months. I left you behind, but you're still in a tough place. Ellen and Howard shouldn't be forgotten.'

'They don't need anyone else. They're so close, you'd think they were the twins.'

'Apart from hormones, you mean?'

'I do.'

'"Stopping by Woods on a Snowy Evening" was a no-brainer.'

'Look kid, so often since you left, I've been speaking "Acquainted with the Night" to myself: "But I have promises to keep / And miles to go before I sleep". I've had some very black nights since you died.'

'So have I. There are signs all over the walls here that say "You can't go back".'

'What do you miss?'

His voice was croaky.

'Mam, Dad, you, my bedroom, my books, my posters and hangings, my cool black clothes. I miss it all.'

'I don't cry so often now. The tears are all gone. But the pain is still there. I replay videos in my head. My favourite recall is the day at Beal Ban when we went snorkelling, but I have one regret.'

'What?'

'We should have gone together, even from a safety point of view.'

'You still have the shell. You have tokens of me near you.'

'Stay until I'm in bed. I'll say goodnight to you then.'

'Benny, be good.'

As soon as our exams were finished, we gazed delightedly at the long, winding road between July and September. Cassie arrived at our house a few days later. She didn't seem herself. Was she back on the vodka?

'It's good news, really,' she said.

'What's happened?'

'Dad's left home. He had the flat above the shop decorated and fitted out. He even has a bedroom for me. As if I need a second bedroom!'

'Are you sad?'

'Yes.'

'Are you vodka-sad?'

'No, Benny, I'm not.'

'How is it with your mam?'

'They're each in great humour. Mam is relaxed and easy. He drops the correspondence for the business over to her when the shop closes. He even stays for coffee and then says goodbye to us.'

'Maybe a bit of time away from each other will do them good.'

'What would do me good right now is fish and chips from the Dainty Fryer.'

I was delighted to accompany her to our favourite eatery. I felt quite adult as we ordered our food. Imagine, we had been doing this for years at the takeaway hatch, but it felt different sitting down and having cutlery.

We began to eat. The fish was divine. The chips were classic – crisp outside and fluffy in the middle. The Diet Coke was ice cold. I was enjoying the food and the chat.

'I have to tell you something.'

I'm not fond of those words. They normally signal something terrible is coming. I decided to breathe.

Cassie put down her cutlery.

'I'm not going to be around for July and August.'

She had the decency to blush, and I was gobsmacked.

'Mam decided I needed a break from all the hassle at home.'

'What about me? Where will you be?'

'I'm going to France. I'm going to mind children and improve my French at the same time.'

'The Leaving Cert is three years away, Cassie. What's the emergency?'

'My mam went to this family when she was a teenager. Benny, you know how tough this year has been for me. Can't you wish me well?'

'I wanted us to be together all summer. We could have cycled up the glen, taken the train to Dublin, gone to a music festival. I wanted to do normal stuff. Don't you want to go camping, drink wine and sneak out of home late at night?'

'All of the above – but you know what home has been like for me. The war of the parents is still going on.'

'I worried about you for months. You were on the vodka and miserable all that time.'

'I worried about you for ages. Since Christopher died, I've tried to be the best support I can. We've become good friends, and I really like you.'

'Why are you going away then? French can wait. You have two whole summers before we go into Leaving Cert.'

Her face changed. She became pale, and sweat beaded her forehead. She looked at me with a cold eye.

A Boat for Benny

'Well, poor old you, whinging like a child. I don't know if you're man enough for me at all. Enjoy your batter. You can have mine, too.'

She walked out with a swagger, her cotton tote bag slung over her shoulder. The chips had cooled, and the batter likewise. The Coke was still drinkable.

'Man up,' Dad said when he got me alone later. 'You're sixteen. This is not forever. She's your first girlfriend, or is she? I was lucky. I met Lila when we were fifteen. It worked for us. It could have been just a summer fling, but it wasn't. Don't become dependent on Cassie. Don't let her become dependent on you. Let her enjoy her summer. Let her off knowing that you have your own plans.'

'But I don't, Dad. I planned to spend loads of time with her.'

'The game has shifted, Benny. Find a new game.'

There was no joy from Mam. She was crocheting a christening shawl.

'If I had wanted to go to France when I was sixteen, I wouldn't have listened to one word from your father. He would have been lucky to get a postcard.'

Ellen was similarly useless.

'I know what's wrong with you. You're just horny. You were hoping for good things over the summer, to have your urges dealt with.'

'I'm pretty sure you've had your urges dealt with for quite a while now.'

'Leave Howard out of this,' she said, banging my bedroom door.

I was still sulking. I remembered the wasted batter and chips. Cassie would be leaving in a few days.

My stubborn part was rigid, and would brook no argument to the contrary.

I called in to see Mrs Mc, who was sitting on the patio.

'All set for the holidays, Benny?'

'I'll be working in the shop.'

'Not all day and all night.'

'True.'

'And your girl is going off to France, a great adventure.'

'I thought she'd stay here with me.'

'Get over yourself. Make sure you wish her well when you say goodbye.'

'Mrs Mc, I'm really fond of her.'

'Why wouldn't you be? She's a lovely girl. I met her when she dropped off the Christmas hampers.'

'Were you and your husband happy?'

'Oh now, Benny, that's very serious. But yes, we were very happy. But I had to think hard about it.'

I sat down because I could feel a story coming.

'I was great with a chap called Dan Daly. He was tall, good-looking and very fit.'

'Sounds good.'

'Well, he was very loud. He talked loudly and laughed loudly and was always in the thick of a crowd. I found it hard to get to know the real person. It felt as if he was acting a part.

'I worked in an office, and one day a young man walked in. He was not too tall or fit, but he spoke quietly and had good manners. He called for me the following Sunday, and we had tea with my mother. He had a decent laugh and was interested in many things, especially reading.

'Dan Daly considered going to England and asked me how I'd feel. We could get married before we went. I didn't want to go to England, and I knew I didn't want to marry Dan. He was surprised, but off he went. So I got to know Sam McCarthy very well. One day, my mother asked me if he was kind. I said, "He is kind and good to me. He is not one for loud chats or guffawing in the streets. He is sincere…" My mother said, "The most important characteristic in a husband is kindness".'

'I took that on board and gave my word to Sam. Dan Daly was all about himself, you see. He liked looking at himself. I took Sam and never regretted it.'

'You tell it very well. I'll be back to mow the lawn on Saturday.'

'God bless you, Benny. You're one of the good ones.'

I swallowed my pride and walked down to say goodbye and wish Cassie 'Bon chance'.

'I hope everything goes well for you.'

'I won't be gone all summer. I'll be back in August.'

I held her in my arms as tightly as I could.

'Cassie, do you know Dire Straits, "Romeo and Juliet"?

'Yes.'

'Maybe our timing is a bit wrong.'

'Oh, Romeo. I used to have a scene with him.'

I stood before her and looked at the girl who made my heart do somersaults. I wanted to ask her to stay. But I let her go.

'I'll see you in August.'

'Yes, have a good summer, Benny.'

And then I ruined it. I couldn't stop myself. It wasn't in the script, so I ad-libbed.

'I love you, Cassie. I think I have loved you since we were three.'

'It's only six weeks. We'll have fun when I get back, n'est pas?'

'À bientôt, ma chérie.'

That night, Christopher arrived.

'So, she's gone to la belle France.'

'Yes, and left without even batting an eyelid.'

'Ah, you played the martyr very well. Did you overdo it a bit?'

'I had plans for the summer. I wanted to spend lots of time together. I'll have my money from the shop. We could have had a great time.'

'Major life lesson, Benny. The world doesn't obey your rules. Plans get changed, re-arranged or cancelled altogether.'

'I know but…'

'Am I a perfect example of the universe scuppering plans? I am.'

'I know.'

'And you didn't fade away from grief. You're still here and making memories since I passed. There is no pause button on life. I see your life move on, and I see you grow physically and in experience.'

'Mam and Dad were no help.'

'Find a new plan. You can't put your life on hold 'til she gets back. Use your time,' he said. 'They don't want to see you moping around. Believe me, they know very well how much you miss me, but they know that you must take every chance that comes your way.

And if you must do without Cassie's company for six weeks, so be it.'

'I agree. I do see that.'

'I'm not going to be here like this forever, Benny. This is borrowed time. I feel some change coming.'

He faded away. I had loads to say, but he wasn't interested in listening. In bed, I went over the conversation. The penny dropped. I can't spend the next six weeks waiting for Cassie to come home. I have to make and execute my own plans. Surely she will have learned plenty while she is away. I must use my time wisely.

I had been without Christopher for eight months now. Christmas had passed, the New Year had come and gone, St Brigid's Day had heralded spring, and St Patrick's Day had reminded us of our Irishness. We had a great time in the West, to the benefit of all. Easter eggs had been consumed, and we had got through the exam season. I had survived, but the gap in my life was still huge. He'd warned me that a change was coming. I don't want to know that, but I believe him. His sadness was more obvious now. There's a feeling of 'last time' in the atmosphere.

Cassie will return, and so will Howard. Christopher has been on the road a long time now. I will have to let him go.

FIFTEEN

We felt free when the exams finished on June 20th. Mam washed and pressed our uniforms. She would sell them on and buy replacements second-hand. She collected all our books and got them ready for re-sale, too. We cleared out our rooms, removed clothes that no longer fit, and prepared to spend the next two months kicking back.

It wasn't all sunshine and fun. Ellen had to do several hours in the shop, and I had to help at the forecourt and in the garage. Dad decided I needed to improve my shop skills, so he put the two of us together for a week. Still, I was not too fond of it, but I watched Ellen. She smiled, carefully checked the scanner, and counted the change. If there was a queue, she kept on smiling. She kept her cool.

If the customers were tired of waiting, she smiled and called out, 'I suppose ye all want 99s. I'll be exhausted, but it's hot today.'

Some people were irate, but most waited in line quietly.

I improved. I could smile as well as anyone. When I realised that the scanner did all the work, I just had to follow the directions on the screen. It even told me the correct change! I still preferred the forecourt and the garage, but the shop was not as frightening as it used to be.

Christopher chuckled.

'I saw you filling 99s and selling cigarettes.'

'Dad insisted that I try new things.'

'Is Ellen going to sweep the forecourt?'

'Stop laughing, Christopher. I doubt it.'

'I notice that Howard makes several visits to the shop daily.'

'Dad had to warn him off. He wasn't buying anything, just ogling his beloved.'

'Says he who would ogle if he could, but can't.'

We both laughed.

'You're surviving anyway?'

'I bought some jeans and a few books. I got the poster of "Starry Night".'

'Put words on what Cassie means to you. I'll ask you next time.'

I avoided the question for ages because I was afraid to think it through. I was comfortable with how I felt about Mam, Dad and Ellen. I didn't need words for that.

How I felt about Christopher, I had already answered. When he was dying, I told him he was my brother.

Though Ellen and I had been womb-mates and had shared that space so well, a drift had started shortly after we were born. She had looked after me so well when Christopher died. Sleeping in her room those few nights was a comfort. She reached down and took my hand when my sorrow almost drowned me. I had the chance to listen when we went out together. To hear that she had her own worries about Howard, and knew that she had taken on too much, showed me that she was another teenager like me. We seemed to swim in different waters day by day, but in a crisis, I knew that she would always be my lifeboat. Though I hadn't yet shown it, I found a firmness in myself to be there for Ellen whenever she might need me.

Cassie was the first person I wanted as a friend. We were only three when she came to our house. She and Ellen made it clear that I was 'outside' the friendship. They had dolls and wouldn't play Duplo or Lego. Ellen wanted Cassie for herself. I was there, but I might as well have been invisible.

When Howard came, it was on a different level. I didn't even know if I liked him, but I wanted to try. There was no plan that he would bring his remote-control car, but what a great idea it was! Though Ellen crashed our cars into each other, all three of us enjoyed the fun.

Early on, the girls began to retreat to Ellen's room. I could hear laughing and jokes from inside, and knew it truly was a 'boy-free zone', just as the sign had said. But I was a boy, and I didn't want to discuss makeup or nail varnish anyway.

Being separated from girls at school had thrown me into friendships with boys. Matt and Howard, two such different creatures, grew on me over time. Matt had a good head for chess and had taught me well. Howard was odd, with his many interests. I thought I had an enquiring mind, but he was interested in everything.

The first time I noticed Cassie as a girl was around Confirmation. She wore a denim dress which suited her. She looked like a girl, and my hormones were on full blast. At home, I watched Ellen and herself together. I observed that she loved jokes, had a loud, warm laugh and could tolerate me. We were thrown together the night she vomited over me. From there, through roundabouts and scary events, we had found our way.

I didn't want to know about her parents' issues. I was deep in mourning for Christopher, and that consumed me. New Year's Eve in her house changed everything – being welcomed into her room, sitting in her leather chair, seeing her books, drawings and posters. I was relaxed there and easy in myself. She had confidence, but like me she was burdened by emotional issues. She wrapped me up in the lovely blanket and read to me. That was a wonderful first. She admitted to liking me for a long time, but never got a chance because I was so taken up with Christopher.

I liked her take on the world: that she would hold my hand secretly, support me in my sorrow, and like me.

I understand my twin better now. I accept Howard as himself, and I will always support Ellen in her life trials. I love Cassie, body and soul – her body and her soul. I want to love her, sleep with her and be a couple, but we're only sixteen. That is all I can give for now.

Once the exams were over, Howard and Ellen changed. They began to wear black clothes, and Ellen began to paint her nails black and wear black lipstick. They were becoming strange.

'Ellen Bernadette, why are your eyes so black?'
'It's new eye shadow.'

'Your eyes look like two holes in a blanket. Are your nails black as well?'

'I'm expressing my approval of the gothic novel.'

'Are you becoming a goth? Justin, she's becoming a goth.'

'I'm just experimenting.'

'I thought all the goths disappeared after the eighties,' Dad said.

'I'm doing my own thing.'

Howard arrived. I had to try very hard not to laugh. His fair, curly hair had been dyed black. He had put soap on it, which made it stand in whirls around his head. He was also wearing eye makeup. Mam kept a straight face.

'What did your mother say, Howard?'

'She's away.'

'And your dad?'

'He said I looked ridiculous, but he remembered some of the stuff he had done when he was my age. He reckons it's a rite of passage.'

'Your mother had this purple dress, I remember,' said Dad.

'Justin, don't go there. Every era has its fashion abominations. Forget it.'

Dad talked about The Cure and Siouxsie and the Banshees. Ellen and Howard listened to him, fascinated. He moved on to Adam and the Ants. Mam groaned. She had loved Adam. She started to laugh.

'Justin, do you remember the girl in St Stephen's Green? She was using an ordinary kettle as a handbag.'

Ellen was angry. 'Laugh away, all of you. If you allowed yourself to wear a dress up to your bottom, leave me alone.'

A Boat for Benny

They moved into her bedroom, and we collapsed laughing.

Still, there was no laughing on Monday morning when she walked into the kitchen with her hair dyed black and several skeleton combs holding it up while tendrils framed her face.

They persisted. The weather was miserable, but the soap made their heads itchy when the warm temperatures arrived, and the black attracted too much heat. Howard had his curls shorn. He was delighted to have a light head again. Ellen let the black grow out. She kept the skeleton combs. In fairness, the long hair suited her. How the dye would behave when she went back to swimming was anyone's guess.

Ellen was shocked when Howard announced he was heading to the States with his dad. Like me, she had planned on spending every available minute of the summer with Howard. They went for four weeks. Ellen bawled for hours when Howard left. I found it strange to see her at a loss. I expected her to have her own plans ready as soon as she knew he was going. For once, she stumbled. My experience was that she glided through life, always on top.

'I love him,' came floating down the stairs. 'I know I act as if I don't care, but I do. I love Howard. I have no one to goth with now that he's away.'

'I'll be your partner,' Dad said. 'I can wear eyeliner with the best of them.'

'Oh, Dad, you're impossible,' she said.

The evening was warm. Ellen fetched a few cans, and Mam arrived out. There was no more talk of love or goths. The Cullens sat on the patio, enjoying the warmth of the dusk.

Howard's dad was giving a paper at a symposium in Washington during the first week. They would then head for Arizona, where a university press had published a pamphlet on Jupiter's Moons by his father, Dr Ibar Bennett. Howard used the time in DC to visit Capitol Hill and the Library of Congress. Arizona was horrendous. Howard emailed about the heat. He said that my limited life experience would prevent me from fully understanding the oppression of the boiling sun. They had imagined that the 'dry heat' would suit them. Howard thanked science for air-con. He spent most of his time cooling off at the shady side of the hotel pool. He would never complain about cold summers again. He hoped Ellen had missed him because he had missed her dreadfully. There were no goths in Tucson. He wasn't surprised though, because of the heat you couldn't wear black, and eyeliner would run down your cheeks.

His dad summed it up thus: 'It was worth the heat to be published, but never again.'

They arrived back at the end of July to rain and gusty winds. Howard swore that he would never again leave the island.

Howard's return caused a stir. It was his ears. The hair and clothes were to be expected, but the holes in his ears were new. Two black rings were inserted into his ear lobes to stretch the skin. That didn't bother Ellen, who cried when she saw him and held onto him all evening. They headed to her room, where he gave her the presents he had brought home. She gave him his welcome home presents – having to do it silently.

'What do you think they're up to, Lila?'

'You know very well what they're at, Justin.'

'Maybe we should draw a line. Remember what your father used to say?'

'No sex below the neck until you're twenty.'

'Ah, the good old days, when Father's word was law.'

The black jeans, which Howard had bought for her, looked exactly the same as the pair she was wearing. The t-shirts were of excellent quality. No one heard about the black underwear he had brought home, or how she modelled it for him. He forgot about Arizona very quickly.

Howard had no money and so signed on for shifts in our shop. He and Ellen always worked different time slots. Dad might be easy and calm, but you could never call him a fool. Of course, they had plenty of time to spend together. They re-dyed their hair and took to the black makeup again.

Dad drew the line.

'It might have been all right for Edward Scissorhands, but you can't work in the shop like that.'

'You can't control our appearance, Dad.'

'Actually, I can. You're not in a union. What I say goes. I've already sacked two for pilfering, and still more are putting their names down. So, decide for yourselves.'

They removed the makeup and wore the standard grey t-shirt. They had to wear hats for health and safety. You could see spikes of jet black here and there at the side of Ellen's head. They read Dracula, Frankenstein and Wuthering Heights to heighten their knowledge of the gothic genre.

SIXTEEN

The house was very quiet. No Cassie laughing in Ellen's room, or sneaking into mine. Howard was far away. He could always be counted on to come up with a bizarre fact or cheer me up with his soaped hair. Ellen and I missed both of them.

I brought her to the Dainty Fryer one evening.

'We never go out together,' she said.

'Always a first time. You're down because Howard is gone, so let me get you a treat.'

'That's decent of you, Benny.'

'Well, remember how good you were to me after Christopher died.'

'I'm glad it helped. You're still deep in grief. I can sense it.'

Was that twin perception? I don't know.

'Are you fond of Howard?'

'I am, but I feel sorry for him too. His home life isn't great.'

'How do you mean?'

'You know his dad is a scientist. His mam is a street performer.'

'A what?'

'She eats fire. Stop laughing, Benny. She works a lot at festivals abroad. Howard spends a lot of time on his own. Even when his dad is home, he works in his office.'

'It must be very different from our house.'

'Why do you think he loves being in our place? It's a warm house with a normal family. Mam and Dad like him. He feels safe there.'

'Do you fancy him, Ellen?'

'A step too far, Benny. Leave it at that.'

'But you must! Ye have been an item for nearly three years.'

'I came here for a bit of peace and quiet. Instead, you're giving me the third degree.'

'I know you're lost without Cassie these holidays. The two of you are so close. I thought you and Howard were close as well. Why be with each other if not?'

'I find it hard to talk about my feelings. You had a truly close relationship with Christopher. The two of you trusted each other completely.'

'We did. He was that kind of person; I could trust him with all my feelings, thoughts and dreams.'

'Howard and I got together early in First Year. You know how much I enjoy being a winner. I was delighted to be one of the first girls to have a boyfriend. Howard is bright, nerdy even, but he is mine.'

'Why all the analysis, Ellen? End it if you want to.'

'I don't know what I want. While he's in the US, I've plenty of time to think. I owe it to him to do that.'

'The two of you spend a lot of time together. He's even welcome in your room.'

'Just leave it, Benny. I'm not good at expressing my feelings the way you are. I don't have that skill.'

'It's not a skill. It's necessary for me to be able

to understand myself. Christopher understood me without any words. He was an old shoe that had grown loose and fitted me perfectly.'

'Well, my friendship with Howard is not on an equal basis. His mother is often abroad, and his work consumes his father. I feel like a mother or an older sister. Howard doesn't get much care at home. He's left to his own devices. The house is more like a doctor's waiting room than a home. The fridge is often empty, and he has to do his own washing. If he has a toothache or an upset stomach, there is no one to make him tea and toast or to hug him. He is crying out for love, but his parents don't seem to notice.'

'You do understand him, Ellen.'

'But I can't supply all his emotional needs, Benny. I'm not his family. We're sixteen, and I want to feel like sixteen and enjoy myself.'

Ellen was more like me than I had realised. She had worries and cares about Howard. She had put herself into a problem-solving role in his life, and it was too awesome a task for her. His parents were nothing like Mam and Dad, who had us at the centre of their lives. This wasn't an equation, which she could have tackled logically and applied mathematical rules to.

'Have you spoken to Mam and Dad?'

'I have, and Cassie. They can all see the problem. I went into a caregiver role too early, and Benny, he is dependent on me now.'

'Look, these weeks away might change the story. He will be with his dad twenty-four-seven. That might bring some good change.'

Our fish and chips arrived.

'Let's leave it now, but thanks for listening.'

'You come into mine any night you need to. You can stay.'

I could feel how she was with Howard and Cassie both gone.

'Cassie will be back in early August. I love it when she stays over. She hugs me when I cry and whispers that all will be well.'

Dad paid us for the hours we worked, and I had an idea for my room. Cassie's leather chair had grown on me.

'Mam, how is that dresser coming on?'

'God, Benny, I've barely made a start. I've had a lot of work on since the New Year. I'm planning on having a run at it in August.'

'I'm going to paint my bedroom and change it around.'

'Go for it.'

'You like old things. Where would I go looking for a leather chair, Mam?'

'Ask Dad where he got the dresser. We can always try Carney Collectibles in Rossmore. I know someone who got a Victorian glass porch from them.'

Carney Collectibles it was. The four of us set out to explore.

'The place is full. From treasures to rubbish, they have everything. Let me do the bargaining if you want something. Have fun,' Dad said.

Mam and I were first in. She had an eye for interesting stuff. I just wanted a leather chair. Ellen was mooching, looking gothic with black eye shadow, a long-sleeved black t-shirt and Doc Martens.

There were plenty of leather chairs. Dining chairs

were of no interest to me. I couldn't afford a modern chair. Dad gave me a wink. I followed him. We went through the showroom, along a passage into an annexe. Only the brave would dare enter.

'This is where I found the dresser,' he whispered. 'I had to clean the dirt off it before I brought it home.'

'Oh, Dad, it's a graveyard for dead furniture.'

'Take it slowly. You could find something special.'

I wished for Christopher. He would have guided me away from the rubbish and towards the stuff with possibilities. I thought of his black leather coat, which was so cool. I almost tripped over a small rug. Had Christopher pushed me?

Then I saw a chair as large as Cassie's chair but in a faded brown. I checked the leather for cuts, places where it had worn away, and stains. I smelt it. I fetched Mam. She told me to take the pieces close to it away. She walked all around the chair, and we tilted it forward.

'It's quite sound, Benny. How much have you to spend?'

'I have eighty euro. I could go to a hundred.'

She called the man.

'I can't do it for less than one twenty,' he said.

'It's fine leather,' Mam said.

'I know that.'

'Pity about the woodworm.'

'There's no woodworm.'

'Indeed there is. Tilt it over there, Benny.'

The wooden base revealed all.

'I suppose I could do it for a hundred so.'

'That woodworm could have invaded some other pieces here. I'd say getting rid of it would be a good idea. We could take it off your hands for seventy.'

They agreed on seventy-five, and Dad would collect it.

'Good choice, Benny,' Ellen said. 'You've seen Cassie's one?'

'Seen it, sat in it and wanted one.'

I needed paint to get started on my room. Cassie's dad came over to me as I searched the shelves.

'Hi, any news from Cassie?' I asked.

'Benny, she's getting on very well. Hasn't she been on to you?'

'Yes, just on WhatsApp, though.'

'She will be back in another few weeks.'

I wanted cream emulsion. Little did I realise that there were at least twenty shades of cream. Her dad helped.

'If you're doing the job yourself, Benny, this paint is very good quality. You'll only need one coat, and it dries quickly.'

The leather chair was taking up a lot of space in the kitchen, but Mam insisted that it go no further until it had been treated for the woodworm. She showed me how to aim the nozzle into the little holes. She insisted that we remove the tacks at the lower edge of the frame.

'Just in case those pests climbed higher.'

I had never painted anything before. Mam told me how to prep. In a few hours, my room looked bright and new. I needed another trip to the paint shop for gloss paint for the door and windowsills. I bought a throw for my bed and cleared the shelves. Only treasured books and photographs remained. I got a large corkboard to display all my photos. Mam proclaimed the chair free of woodworm, and it was placed under the window. There were no trees, but the church in the distance would be my focal point.

On July 20th, Mam and Dad took us to The Italian Connection for our birthday. We were delighted to be sixteen. We had a glass of wine each and chose pizza. For dessert, we all had ice cream. Ours came with swizzles and a candle. The waiter sang Happy Birthday.

I gave Ellen some swimming togs. She would be on the senior swim team in September, and I knew that chlorine had a bad effect on togs. Mam helped me choose one that was chlorine-resistant. I would say Mam also had a hand in what Ellen got me. I know that Tom Brown's Schooldays was written long ago, but Mam knew I wanted to read it.

I was excited and nervous to unroll Christopher's painting. He'd said that in my painting, the sky would decide everything. I laid his gift on my study table.

The sun shone. White, puffy clouds barely moved. The ripples on the water pulled you in towards the boat. I could see myself. Christopher was beside me. We were both smiling. The caption read, 'There will always be a place for you in my boat, Benny. Happy Birthday.'

Cruel life to have taken him away! He would never see my leather chair, the freshly painted walls or the new throw on my bed. I cried, then. His loss sat heavily in my chest. We should have been laughing together. We should have howled at the contrast in our work. My picture was full of foreboding, his of happiness.

A Boat for Benny

I rolled it up, and walked to his house.

'Benny, come in,' Tess said.

Andy appeared from the sitting room.

'How are you, Benny?'

'It was my birthday yesterday.'

'Happy Birthday.'

'I should be asking how the two of you are.'

Tess busied herself with the kettle. Even from the back, I could see her pain. She had stopped dyeing her hair. A grey plait hung to her shoulder blades.

'I could lie and say we're coping, but we're not. We miss him every single day. We miss his laughter and his smiles. He was so talented. He could have done anything.'

'We wanted him to have every chance.'

Tess poured the tea and buttered the scones, but none of us moved.

'He was a great friend to me.'

'You were a great friend to him.'

'Don't be shocked, but I think I hear him sometimes. I thought what happened at Christmas was a once-off, but he whispers to me occasionally.'

'We hear him too.'

I showed them his painting. They cried and laughed at the caption.

'I needed to know we would be in a boat together. But I have to sail alone now.'

'I think he will always be with you, Benny.'

'I wanted him here, not in a picture. I still want him to come back to me.'

They kept quiet, but I could feel the sobs brewing.

'There's a big gaping hole inside me, and nothing fills it. I'm never going to see him again. I'm bereft.'

The three of us sat and cried. We were cross then, and derided the powers that be for not keeping him safe on his way home.

'Sometimes I'm cross with Cassie. If she hadn't been sick, I would have stayed at the hop, and he and I would have walked home together, same as always. Same as always.'

I lay down on the couch, and they put a rug over me. I must have fallen asleep. When I awoke, I could hear 'Starry, Starry Night' playing in the kitchen. I wanted to howl, but what came to me was a smile.

'Would you like to go up to his room, Benny?'

'No, not this time. Could I come back again and visit?'

'Of course. You're welcome here anytime.'

'You know I'm a twin.'

'Yes. Your sister is the swimmer.'

'I don't know if we're close at all. We seem to live in different life zones.'

'You were together from the beginning.'

'Yes, and she was really kind to me when Chris died. They were alike in many ways.'

'What do you mean, Benny?'

'They were both brave. Ellen isn't fearful, and neither was Chris. She got all the bravery, and I got all the anxiety.'

'We all have faults and weaknesses, Benny.'

'Christopher was brave, and he wasn't afraid.'

'And now he is no more.'

'We heard about the Transition Year musical.'

'He would have loved that.'

They both wept. Tess put her head in her hands and cried. Andy stood looking out at the back garden.

A Boat for Benny

'Just to have him back for five minutes, to see him feed the birds. Oh God, my lovely boy, my son.'

I slipped out. I hoped they would hold each other. Their only hope was to hang on tight to one another. There were black days ahead of them, and a lifetime of tears.

SEVENTEEN

The weather for the August Bank Holiday was awful. In wintertime, that leaden grey in the sky is a sign that there will be snow, but in August, it means that heavy rain is on its way and that thunder may follow. I disliked this kind of sky. I felt that the ceiling had fallen down and was barely a few inches above my head.

'There's not a breath of air. A downpour is what we need to clear that,' I whispered to myself.

It rained non-stop. A drear wind blew down from the mountain. People stayed indoors. On Sunday afternoon, we were watching the All-Ireland Hurling Semi-Final. Ellen opened the door, expecting the man with the holey ears. I heard whispering.

Cassie was right there. Looking very tanned and healthy, she arrived in the room. I grabbed her and hugged her close to me. We crept out of the room, giggling.

In the kitchen, I hugged and kissed her, touched her hair and kissed her eyes. I cried then, making a right fool of myself. I showed her my bedroom. The new paint met with her approval.

'A leather chair, almost as old as my own,' she said, and smiled.

'Your room really reflected you, so I wanted my room to be calm, have books, my pictures, and welcome me every time I entered.'

I didn't say that I wanted Christopher to feel easy and safe. Neither did I mention the top of the wardrobe, which had been given a coat of white chalk paint and looked ten times better than it had.

'How was France?'

'Great, yes. My French has really improved. The children were lovely, but I don't want to work with children.'

'Still the figures?'

'Yes, Benny. I have to wait for results, but I'm sure I want to work in finance. I love Maths.'

'With Transition Year coming up, we will all have a breathing space. The Leaving Cert is three years away. How are things at home?'

'As they were. Dad is still in the flat. Mam is in the house. Peace seems to reign over all.'

'Lie down,' I said.

'Say please,' she said.

'Please lie down on my bed. I will put the new quilt over you, as you did in your room for me. I want to read you something.'

I wrapped her with the quilt, and I lay beside her. I had chosen the poem especially. It wasn't aimed at Cassie. I was speaking to the universe but hoping she would understand.

'He wishes for the Cloths of Heaven' left us silent for several minutes. I thought she had fallen asleep, but a hand slipped into my hand.

She whispered, 'Tread softly on my dreams, too, Benny.'

As I lay in bed that night, the wind was still howling, and the rain was battering the window. It was cold for August. I needed a blanket. I got one from the top of the wardrobe. A photo of Christopher floated down. I placed it beside his painting, above my bed.

'I hardly knew the room when I arrived.'

He was back!

'I had a bit of a makeover. You were away for ages.'

'The longer you have passed, the less time they give you down here.'

'Cassie is back from France.'

'I observed the shenanigans earlier.'

'That was private!'

'Benny, who would I tell?'

'Christopher, I'm finding it hard without you. I thought we would be men together.'

'Old pal, I'm fading fast. I will try to last until after the musical. I want to enjoy the show from the wings.'

'I've missed you loads. Sometimes I talk to you, even when you're nowhere near.'

'People talk to God like that. They trust that He is near. He could be in Outer Mongolia or at the tip of South America. Distance is nothing to the deity. It only takes an instant for me to get here.'

'Why have you been missing for so long?'

'I'm not supposed to be here at all. I'm due to move on. But my folks are so sad. You've seen them. My mam has circles under her eyes, and my dad is stooped over. The life has gone out of them since I died. You were fairly bad yourself the last day.'

'Have you any advice for me, Chris?'

'A dead man has no advice. I only know that there is a journey ahead of me. This is not goodbye, Benny.

I will be back. I will.'

'Will there be room for me in your boat, Chris?'

'Always.'

EIGHTEEN

The last two weeks in August were glorious. The sun shone. Though a pesky breeze kept the temperatures down, it was dry and clear. The four of us had great fun. We were all relaxed. The prospect of Transition Year held no fears of exams.

We went to the cinema, had meals, and took the bus to Quarryside for the hurdy-gurdies, the big wheel and the chair-o-planes. We had picnics, hiked through the glen and watched repeats of Black Books.

Howard's mam had returned from Amsterdam. When she saw the holes in his ears, there was pure murder in her eyes.

'What do you think you're doing, Howard?'

'I got them done in America. It is part of my goth statement.'

'I'll give you a goth statement!'

'Mam, you have dreads in your hair. Is that not you making a rasta statement?'

'Ibar, you let him do this to himself. What were you thinking? And the soap in his hair! I could scream.'

'He knows he can't wear the rings in school. They will be out by the end of August.'

'They'll be out by tomorrow. You're seeing the doctor, mister.'

A Boat for Benny

Howard arrived at our house in a state of woe.

'The doctor! I have to have my rings removed. She will make me have stitches. Imagine!'

All parents have limits. You can test that limit, but experience taught me that playing it safe near home is best.

I don't think I would manage well with a mother who spends a lot of time away from home. I can tell when Mam is in the house. Some intuition lets me know that she is present. I don't mind about the knitting. Mam can talk, listen to Irish verbs, call out a list for the supermarket and ask for a cup of tea without ever losing a stitch or having to repeat a row. She also knows when a loud voice is needed with teenagers, and when silence is the key. She says very little when I am sad or lonely, but sits beside me on the couch. She knows you need a clean shirt to take your girl out. She never cleans your room but lets you know when she wants it done. She insists on bedlinen being changed every two weeks. She knows that young people need privacy. She follows her own dreams and spends time as she chooses.

You would never refer to Mam as a housewife. She's a woman. She has a mortal fear of STIs and teenage pregnancy. She would be surprised how far away from those her twins are. Dad services cars. They work as a team. She is not a street entertainer. She has no tats. It would be fine if she did. She doesn't wear dreads, real or otherwise.

Howard was able to remove the rings himself. His lobes hung down and flapped. His mam screamed when she saw them. She marched him off to the doctor. Dr Fennelly had dealt with us all since we were small. He smiled and then laughed.

'You'll put in a few stitches, doctor, to get him sorted.'

'Now, Sandy, let's be reasonable.'

'He hasn't been reasonable. His father hasn't either. Things go mad when I'm away.'

The doctor said nothing. He thought to himself that Sandy had driven her parents mad when she was young. He examined Howard's ears.

'I'll just give the lobe area a good wash with disinfectant, Howard. You removed the circles yourself, did you?'

He was a gentleman and soon completed his task.

'Now, about getting rid of the holes…' Sandy said, determined.

'I'll put steri-strips at the back of your ear lobes, Howard, if that's alright?'

'That's fine, doctor. I couldn't wear the circles to school anyway.'

'I want the holes gone,' Sandy insisted.

'Now, Sandy, if I remember correctly when you were sixteen, you decided to get your belly button pierced. Your mother had to bring you here because the piercing became infected. You spent a few nights in hospital because your temperature was so high. Howard's lobes are perfectly clean. There is no sign of any infection. Change the steri-strips once weekly, Howard, and see me in two months.'

Howard was happy with the doctor's plan. His mam was livid. Not only would Dr Fennelly not do as she asked, but he had given Howard information that he might use in the future.

He enjoyed telling us the tale. I had never realised

A Boat for Benny

what a good actor he was. He had us in stitches, looking over his glasses like the doctor did. He pouted like his mam and showed us his steri-strips. He produced the rings from his pocket and said, 'Listen, folks, I don't think I'll be putting these in again next summer. It was a bit of fun this year, but my lobes wobble like earrings.'

It was indeed true. He shook his head, and his lobes reminded us of elephant ears. He began to laugh, and we all joined in. We cheered for him then. Ellen and Cassie decided that they were never getting piercings. I was in favour of keeping my body au naturel.

NINETEEN

The Junior Cert, and the loss of Christopher, had taken their toll on me. I rejoiced in the fact that I would have three full years before the Leaving Cert raised its head.

Transition Year, quite a new invention, would help me draw breath and morph into a cool, laid-back guy, ready to grab all the happiness and fun this time would give. The prospects were to my liking: the musical, work experience and the trip to Paris.

My sense of floating like Ophelia on the river of ease was quickly dispelled when aptitude tests were mentioned. It made sense that they would want to find out what kind of brains we had and what we would thrive on. The results would also highlight what areas of employment or study would not suit us.

Transition Year provides an 'alternative' way to learn. Students get the chance to learn in different ways. On the PE curriculum, there are chances to learn orienteering, rock climbing and even dancing! There is a big input into social studies and citizenship. We first tasted that with the Christmas trees the previous year, and now there would be more.

The first term highlight of the Transition Year was the school musical. Transition students would act, sing, dance, do props and costumes and prepare the school hall. Your contribution to the show's success would count towards passing the year. In the second term, we would have work experience. A report would be given by the employer who took us on. We would also have an intensive course in Computer Studies, which had to be passed.

We started as a group of two hundred and forty students in the First Year, but we were now a mere sixty. Some people couldn't wait to be sixteen in order to leave the place.

Some left to take up an apprenticeship. A large group, whose parents didn't believe in Transition Year, put them straight into Fifth Year. Some went to boarding school, moved away, or transferred to the Institute.

When the school reopened at the end of August, our task was to shepherd the First Years around the school. We were unpaid security. We got them into their base classrooms for roll call. When their tutors left, we guided them to their next station. We waited outside that room to move them on their way again. Sometimes, we had to help a small fellow who was overwhelmed by the numbers in the corridors. If I chanced not to spot something, Christopher whispered in my ear and pointed it out. He was an expert on chaps who might be bullied. I believed that I would spot the bully-fodder easily myself – small and thin, small and fat, pale-skinned or freckled, red-haired, possibly wearing glasses, snuffling and looking terrified.

I found a tall, heavy fellow in the bicycle shed. He was shivering. I walked him around the yard, got a glass of milk and a scone, and sat with him until he calmed down.

'I'm in Transition Year,' I said. 'I'll meet you at the gate at nine on the dot tomorrow morning. I'll walk in with you and show you the school's layout. How does that sound?'

'That would be great,' he mumbled.

'I'll put my number into your phone. If you feel afraid at any stage, text me. Transition students are on "buddy duty" for the next two weeks. I'm Benny, and I'll be your buddy if you like.'

'I'm Martin Kavanagh,' he said.

Ellen and Cassie were fearsome, protecting the new girls. Having spent the last eight years away from boys, they had forgotten what education with boys could mean. Their poor noses were assaulted by the smell of too much (or not enough) deodorant, and ripe farts. The real danger was from older girls who were bigger than them, and much cooler. The amount of money extracted from First Year girls in September was legendary. Most of this extortion was done by Junior Cert girls who had been robbed themselves two years previously. Ellen and Cassie found the poor creatures hiding in the toilets. A pale face streaked with tears, a skirt to her ankles and an air of despair said it all. The girls got to know them, walked home with them and saved their mobile numbers. They told the young ones to text if they had any trouble.

Swimmers have great upper-body strength. How Ellen separated the Third Years from the money they had forced from the First Years took more than strength. If the little ones were intimidated that they would be beaten up on the way home, they told Ellen and Cassie, who quickly put that to bed.

Let us not pretend that we were knights and ladies in shining armour. Of course, there was smoking behind the shed, dashing down to Mrs Mooney's shop at lunchtime and getting ready for the highlight of the first weekend back, the Results Hop in the Marian Hall.

Ellen had a great result. Her grades were all As or Bs. Howard's were similar. Cassie was happy with her results, and though her French grade was low, her few weeks there during the summer should have helped her believe in herself. I got mostly Cs, but was thrilled with As in English and History.

The Results Hop was a mixed blessing for me. Of course there was much to celebrate, but Christopher was gone. He would certainly have gotten As in English, Art and Woodwork. I could feel him on my shoulder. He was very down. He had wanted to be one of us, getting our exam results. He had never planned on being dead.

Howard and I walked up together. Ellen had gone down to Cassie's house to get ready. I knew which jeans and shirt I would wear, and how I was going to gel my hair. I didn't need Howard beside me to help with decisions. In fairness, Christopher was on top of the wardrobe while I got ready.

'Plan nothing. I know you will be meeting the beloved Cassie. This is a fun night for everyone. It's not the time to swear undying love to anyone. On no account give her alcohol. You know she can't handle it. Keep your tongue in your mouth and enjoy dancing with her.'

Howard was all in black. He had washed his hair

and left his face without makeup. We thought about having a few cans outside the handball alley, but that thought was quashed when we remembered Mr Conroy was at the door.

Derek McMc was spinning the discs. It was quite dark in the hall. You could see people, but it brought a sense of intimacy to a big, open space. The lights would be full on as soon as Mr Conroy finished door duty. He knew how to supervise a hop.

My mind returned to Halloween: Cassie being drunk, vomiting over my shoes and chinos, and bringing her home. The next day, hearing of Christopher's condition, the news that he would not survive and had only days left.

We danced fast and slow. We played air guitars, doing the splits to suit. We romanced our girls to the slow music sets. We were just sixteen and having a ball. The four of us headed back to our house, to heat up pizzas and chips and open bottles of Heineken.

Howard and Ellen left us, and we took the two-seater.

'Will we?' Cassie whispered.

'The same again?' I asked, surprised.

'Why change a winning formula?' said Cassie.

We watched three more episodes of Black Books.

The girls slept together, and Howard walked home.

TWENTY

Aptitude tests give a profile of you as a person. Suppose you are colour-blind – marine engineering or being an electrician is not an option. A phobia about blood cuts you off from medicine or nursing. They put all your answers into the computer, programme in your Junior Cert results, and then you go in for the interview.

Mr Matthews and Miss Clancy welcomed me in. They complimented me on my exam results, and on helping the older people at Christmas. They said I had behaved well in the West.

'You're what we call an "all-rounder".'

'I'm aware of that. I get on with my work, but nothing makes me sparkle.'

'Are you interested in business at all?' Miss Clancy wondered.

'Not in the slightest. I help in the garage at weekends, but it's not for me. I sweep up and keep an eye on the forecourt. I'm hopeless in the shop. My sister is brilliant. She has a good manner with people, but I have no small talk.'

'But you're well able to get on with older people. Your work at Christmas was great,' Mr Matthews said.

'I can't go into an area where people will look at me. My sister is a bright star. I like to get on and do my bit in the background.'

'You seem to compare yourself to your twin a lot. Why is that?'

'Ellen was born first. She is the brave one. I trust her completely. In Germany, they say about trust, "I would steal horses with him". I would steal horses with Ellen.'

'Benny, we have some options based on your aptitude results.'

'Forester?'

'No.'

'Librarian, Garda, vet, technician?'

'Nothing appeals.'

'What time did you enjoy best at primary school?'

'I loved being in Infants with Miss Atkins. I had a great time in Third and Fourth Classes because Mr O'Toole got me interested in reading. When he read The Hobbit aloud, I was hooked.'

'Have you considered teaching?' Miss Clancy asked.

'I haven't thought of it. I would have empathy for the shy, anxious ones. I'd love to bring out the best in all the children.'

'Children are easy to talk to. You have to be yourself. You don't have to be the world's best anything.'

'Right then. You'll do your work experience in the boys' school. Miss Atkins is still teaching Infants. She's looking forward to seeing you.'

'How did you know that I would say yes to teaching?'

'Take a look at the printout.'

I did so, and the paper read: The best choice of career for this student is Primary Teaching.

'Thanks,' I said, and smiled the whole way home.

TWENTY ONE

Ellen was told that trying for medicine would be a great choice for her. Howard's IQ was very high, and he would have the pick of university courses. It was suggested that working independently in a research setting would play to his strengths. Cassie's aptitude for figures would open up accountancy and finance for her. She was delighted.

We had great chats over the chip dinner that Friday. We were floating just below the ceiling – as if the Junior Cert results have anything to do with the Senior Cycle! It was lovely to bask in the glow for a little while.

By October 1st, the rumblings about the musical had begun. Auditions were tough for The Boy Friend. So many of the girls wanted the main part of Polly Brown, the competition was fierce. Ellen was chosen. James Hourigan was the main man. He played Tony. Cassie would play Mme. Dubonnet, with a decent French accent. I chose to be in charge of sets and set changes, and had three people to help me.

Howard was asked to work on logistics, since his

computer skills were legendary. He was tasked with liaising between all the groups to ensure everything worked smoothly for the five performances.

By mid-October, we were rehearsing every afternoon. I had to be there to organise the set changes. Once they got their costumes, they played Charleston music at home and danced away. One night, Mam got me to gel my hair and wear Dad's suit trousers with braces. I became part of the scene. The white shirt was crisp and clean. The cloth in the trousers was fine. We laughed and sang, shimmied and swung.

'I could be happy with you, if you could be happy with me.'

We might stay in this bubble of delight forever. We could pretend that The Boy Friend was real life. The girls could wear flapper dresses and feathers in their hair. Howard and I could wear blazers and boaters and carry walking canes. There would be 'lights, camera, action' for every new scene.

Christopher had plenty to say about living in a bubble. He warned me about living in an imaginary world.

'Life doesn't come wrapped in fancy paper. You must look into your situation and face its issues and limitations.'

'How did you get so wise for a young fellow?'

'Being dead gives me a whole new perspective. I'll be there for opening night, though I'll be invisible in the wings. I'd have loved to play Tony.'

'You would have been great. The dancing would be no bother to you. I'm thinking of how you were at the céilí dancing in Muiríoch.'

'Looking back again, Benny. What is the point? You

have lived almost a whole year without me. You've had a whole twelve months of life without this old pal.'

'I'm trying everything to keep your memory alive. I replay our adventures over and over in my head. As long as I can see us with my inside eye, I know you are still close.'

'Look, I want you to put your best effort into the musical. Be busy, be involved, be full on.'

'I wonder if I made you up. Are you just a projection of my brain, because I'm so sad that you're gone?'

'The coffee machine was very hot on Christmas Eve,' he said.

I smiled.

Cassie waited for me after rehearsal. She was leaning against the wall of the bicycle shed, looking glum.

'You won't believe it.'

'What?'

'My mother is pregnant.'

'How could she be?'

'It seems he was over and back when I left for France. One night, he didn't go back.'

'Is he at home for good?'

'He is now. They told me this morning, and I'm so embarrassed.'

'You should be glad they're back together, Cassie.'

'After what they put me through, Benny?'

'I think you should be delighted for them.'

'How would you like it if your mam was pregnant?'

'I wouldn't, but my mam is forty-five. Your mam is still young.'

'After nearly a year of fighting, they patched things

up so easily.'

'Be happy for them.'

'I think I'll move into the flat on my own.'

'Let's enjoy the next few weeks of The Boy Friend. Come on.'

She was still bothered.

There was no chance of the flat, since her dad had already rented it out. He'd said that the new baby would need a lot of stuff, so better to save the rent money.

He was whistling around the place like there was no tomorrow.

TWENTY TWO

Five nights!

We had to turn up for school but could do little during daylight hours. We cleaned and swept the hall every morning. We were astonished at the amount of sweet papers, Coke cans and apple cores. There were sweets stuck to the floor, and that tacky feeling left behind by spilt fizzy drinks.

The chairs were locked together in blocks of ten, making the work easier. The school cleaners had enough to do with their everyday work. We needed rubber gloves and plenty of bleach for the toilets.

Raffle prizes were collected from the storeroom. The good prizes needed to be spread over the five nights. The town businesses gave worthwhile stuff. Some parents had donated bottles of cheap wine – no one wanted to win them.

Howard's spreadsheets were a joy to behold. Every morning, he provided a printout for the different groups. He always had a Plan B. By Friday afternoon, the atmosphere all over the school was electric. This was the finale, and everyone was required to put in their very best effort. Costumes were repaired and pressed, shoes were shined, and new tights were acquired.

I did a final check of the props and the sets. I was quicker now than I had been on Monday. My team flitted on and off the stage in a matter of moments.

The cast lifted their game. The singing and dancing were spot on. We all ran onstage for the final rendering of 'I Could Be Happy with You'.

The backstage crew were called. Howard took a bow. The audience rose as one and clapped us for what seemed like ages. The final round of the raffle included the bottles of cheap wine, but Mam was lucky to win a tin of Afternoon Tea biscuits. Dad won a bottle of whiskey, and I won a fish supper for two.

Everyone gathered in the lunch room for tea and cake. Christopher's parents were there. I was so glad to see them, especially since they looked a bit better.

'He would have loved it,' Eithne said.

'He was able to sing, you know,' added Andy.

'I can imagine the fine sets he would have painted, but I can imagine him acting as well.'

'It was a great production. Your sister has a lovely voice, and your girl's French accent was spot-on.'

'We're heading back to America for Christmas. Will you put that snowman on your tree again?'

'You can't face Christmas without him?'

'Not here, in our own house. The place is so quiet without him.'

'I will, close to my own.'

We took our time getting home. We were happy and light-hearted. The show had been a great success. We swiped some Pinot Grigio on the way out. The teachers had decided some bottles couldn't be raffled.

A group of us headed for The Cutting. Robbing the wine wasn't the thrill we thought it would be. We had no containers, so had to swig from the bottle. Not exactly a rip-roaring thrill.

I walked Cassie home. We sauntered along in delicious silence. I went in for tea. It took us twenty minutes to say goodnight. I would have to do a few hours at the garage, but we would have the fish supper on Saturday evening.

I presented the voucher, and we ordered our food.

'Instead of having supper here, let's return to my house – I have a free gaff.'

My heart was beating fast. Things were happening in my boxers, and possibilities were rearing their heads. Idiot! I started to think of vodka. She might have been planning on having a few. If her folks came back, would I be blamed? Would she be sick over me again?

We got plates, cutlery and glasses. No vodka bottle was produced, and we drank Diet Coke. We sat on the couch and watched Black Books. The chips were delicious, and the fish was cooked perfectly.

Cassie took off her shoes then, and put on fluffy socks.

We watched a tense French thriller. It was an old black and white one. The costumes were from the forties. You know those movies where the women have painted on eyebrows, wear a hat over one eye and do sexy smoking? It was going on in the background, since there was a much better thriller taking place on the couch. There was no smoking or hats and, to my knowledge, the eyebrows were Cassie's alone.

There was lots of kissing, stroking hair, whispering, touching stomachs and exploring. I was in heaven. Cassie seemed to be floating in her own cosmos. I didn't want her to think I was dying to do it. I was, but I didn't know the first thing about practicalities.

Cassie took charge.

'We're not doing it anytime soon.'

'Okay.'

'I'm not ready yet.'

'Okay.'

'Mam's bump is beginning to show. I get nervous when I think it could happen to me.'

'We will have to take precautions.'

'I'll go on the pill.'

'You can't get it until you're eighteen.'

'Listen, Benny, half the town is on it. All you have to do is tell the doctor you have very heavy periods, and bingo, you're handed a script.'

I buttoned my shirt and tucked it into my jeans. Cassie sorted her underwear, and we got our shoes. When her folks got home, we were playing cards.

'I hope you behaved yourselves,' her mam said.

'No wanton sex around here, Mother.'

'Well I hope not, young lady. Goodnight, Benny.'

We lingered on the doorstep.

'You got to eat all your batter tonight,' she whispered.

'And my chips.'

'And then you had dessert,' she giggled.

'Goodnight to ye,' I laughed. 'I'll see you in my dreams.'

As Christmas arrived, I again volunteered for the

A Boat for Benny

Christmas trees. Howard came with me this time. Meeting Mrs Mc was like meeting an old friend. We went through the same ritual. We had the tea, moved the side table, wrapped the ornaments and put them away. She tried to figure out who Howard was. All he could tell her was that they were blow-ins.

Mr O was like a different man. He would be going to Mrs Mc for Christmas again this year. This time, he was supplying the turkey and ham. The potatoes were from his garden. The primary schools had asked him to start growing vegetables on the premises. The classes loved to go out and help him.

Our own Christmas was lovely. We did the usual: drank the toast to absent friends, hung Christopher's snowman close to mine, and visited his grave on Christmas Day. This time, I visited him alone. His anniversary had passed, and the grief was not so traumatic now. I closed my eyes briefly and hoped he would be standing beside me when I opened them.

He wasn't.

Cassie invited us for hot chocolate and biscuits on Christmas morning. The house was full of Christmas. There were plenty of good tidings and carols. Her dad was doing all the prep and the cooking. Her mam's bump was quite big now. She was resting on the couch with her feet up.

'When is your baby due?' asked Howard.

'Early March. But babies have a mind of their own. They come when they're ready.'

'You have a big gap,' he continued.

'That's life,' she said. 'But I don't think we'll be going again.'

Cassie's face was red with embarrassment. Ellen

stared Howard down and made throat-cutting gestures to warn him off. We followed Cassie upstairs. The girls took the bed, I bagged the leather chair. Howard sat at the table.

'I'm sorry, Cassie. I was only making conversation.'

'Don't worry. I feel embarrassed about the pregnancy. I don't know anyone my age whose mother is pregnant.'

'Are ye coming to ours tonight?'

'Have ye plenty of trifle?' Howard wanted to know.

'We have.'

'I'm staying at home tonight with the folks,' said Cassie.

'See you tomorrow,' we said.

TWENTY THREE

The New Year arrived. We would have classes for four weeks, and then head out for work experience. They talked about being polite, not going into staffrooms or kitchens unless invited, and keeping any observations to ourselves.

I was delighted to be heading back to the boys' school. I was so happy to be seeing Miss Atkins and Mr O'Toole. I knew that Mr O'Toole was the principal now. There would be new teachers, of course, and I'd heard an extension had been built since my day.

I knocked at the office door and was called in. Mr O'Toole was a shadow of his former self. A man who had once stood tall and easy, and met life with a healthy smile, had disappeared. In his stead was a man burdened by work. His hair was grey, and his face had a haunted look. He welcomed me and handed me several sheets of paper.

'You're welcome back, Benny. We're delighted to see you.'

'I'm glad to be back, Mr O'Toole.'

'I know that you're supposed to be in classrooms all the time, but I will have to amend that, Benny. The caretaker is in hospital, and things have fallen behind in the past few weeks. I'll need you for caretaking duties on Tuesdays and Thursdays, and for emergencies.'

Before I could get to Miss Atkins' class, I needed to empty all the rubbish into the big wheelie bins and take them to the front of the school. Next, the PE equipment needed to be sorted. The teachers sent children to me for what was required. Percussion instruments were also needed.

The secretary was busy with Confirmation booklets, so I had to take over the photocopying for a few hours. By lunchtime, I had completed the tasks for that day. The Infants finished early, so I had no time to call on Miss Atkins.

In the afternoon, there was an incident in Room Eight – and I now know how unpleasant cleaning up vomit is. At two p.m., Mr Evans sent for me. The sink was blocked, and someone had let the tap run. The children were squealing with delight. Some child had deliberately stuck a roll of tissue into the plughole. I decided to say nothing to Mr Evans.

I was all set to go to Miss Atkins on Wednesday, but it was not to be. Miss Geary requested that I go to her room. There were some disruptive children in her class. One boy spent most of his time under the table. A little girl hummed to herself constantly.

'Can I take the boy under the table out for a few minutes?'

'Out? Out where?' Miss Geary responded.

'He could help me sort the PE equipment,' I said, winking.

The little boy was very keen. The children were busy with an activity when we returned to the classroom.

A Boat for Benny

The boy told Miss Geary that 'the man' would help him catch up. At lunchtime, I asked her about the little girl who hummed.

'It's a coping strategy. Her daddy has a drinking problem, and there are many rows at home. She hums to drown out the noise.'

'I can't come back tomorrow, miss. I have caretaker duties.'

'Sometimes a child needs a hug, but we can't do that anymore.'

'You're doing a great job, miss. There are very needy children here.'

By Friday, I was finally able to spend time with Miss Atkins.

The children in Miss Atkins' class were well-behaved and got on with their work. I took my life in my hands and mentioned Miss Geary's class.

'Sometimes life throws up a class where several children have issues. It could be problems at home, unemployment, a sick child, or a grandparent. Whatever the trouble, it lodges in a little head.'

The children painted rainbows. Brian, who had needed help colouring in the number three, needed no help with painting. He used three colours: black, white and orange.

'I'm saving the bright colours for a seaside picture during the summer,' he said.

The two weeks flew by, and my best experience by far was in Miss Atkins' room.

She said, 'You will make a great teacher, Benny. You have that most important quality.'

'Which is?'

'Empathy, young man – empathy.'

'You have it in spades, miss. Didn't you call me a superhero when I was five?'

'Ah, you and your huge wings.'

'Do you remember Christopher, miss?

'Indeed I do. He was very quiet but already good at Art. I'm sorry, Benny. I know he was your friend.'

'You gave him the part of a star in the Christmas play. He had a tummy bug and missed it.'

'Imagine a nativity scene without a star! With big classes, I had to be creative.'

'I have his snowman. I put it on our Christmas tree with my own. His one still has the two black eyes and all its cotton wool.'

When my time was up, I called into the office to thank Mr O'Toole for taking me.

'The teachers were delighted with you, Benny. You were a great help to me filling in for the caretaker, too.'

'Mr O'Toole, you look very tired.'

'It's a very different job to teaching a class, Benny.'

'You were a brilliant class teacher, sir. We all remember The Hobbit and The Lion, the Witch and the Wardrobe. I developed a love of reading in your class.'

'I'm not really a files and forms kind of man. I enjoy being with the children and seeing them develop. All this office work doesn't suit me.'

'I wish you all the best, Mr O'Toole. I would give you "excellent" for everything.'

He shook my hand and wished me well.

At the end of the two weeks, we were interviewed. I mentioned my time in the boys' school, how perceptive Miss Atkins had been and still was, the giant wings I had for the play, Mr O'Toole reading The Hobbit to us. Miss Atkins had just gotten better over the years. Miss Geary had a difficult class. At the end of the two weeks, I greatly empathised with her. Mr O'Toole should have stayed in the classroom, where his skills were much better suited.

They asked me why I would choose this career.

'I would choose it because I think I would be good with the weak ones. I met a little boy with poor muscle development. He's waiting for a physio appointment. There's another child who spends his time under the table, a little girl who hums non-stop and another who talks to himself all day. Those three are waiting on a psychological assessment to get help.'

'Miss Clancy, he went out a teenager.'

'Mr Conroy, he has come back a man.'

Howard, meanwhile, invented a new way of inventorying the fruit and vegetables in Tesco. Management was impressed. He then studied the amount of strain it put on workers to lift such heavy boxes. He sourced a pedal lift for handcarts. The workers became more efficient, and their fitness improved. Howard lost weight. No one in Fruit and Veg was calling him a geek now. Howard had discovered that science can be applied everywhere.

Cassie's two weeks in Acton West Accountants were a great success. She worked efficiently, asked for help, was polite and admitted her mistakes. Mr Acton told her she had the brain and the temperament for accountancy. He would have a summer job for her.

Ellen was sent to the nursing home. She was not pleased. She offered to sing and dance for the residents. Help was needed with getting people to the toilet, feeding them and taking them for a walk around the grounds. She read for some and wrote letters for others. By the second week, she was cleaning anyone who dribbled their food, wiping noses and singing. They requested old songs. She brought in a group from The Boy Friend, and they did an excerpt from the show. She was asked to return for their carol service at Christmas.

Dead people have no work experience. I wondered about an aptitude test for Christopher. Perhaps they would have sent him to a graphics studio or to work with a photographer. He would have loved the library. Being near books had always been a joy for him.

I would ask him, if he contacted me again.

TWENTY FOUR

The Easter holidays were only days away. We were flying on Holy Thursday, and would land in Beauvais. Ellen and I had our wages from the shop. There was great speculation about which teachers would be travelling. Mrs O'Driscoll was hoped for. She was sorry but had to have her veins done during the break. Miss Clancy's only virtue was that she believed in a late breakfast, and wouldn't be bullied. She was going. The chances of an open fire and shadows on the ceiling were limited, but the prospect of more of Mr McCullough's ghost stories was a great hope for everyone. Oh, joy! He said yes.

Mr Matthews' divorce hearing was scheduled for the following Tuesday, so he was not available. Someone from management would have to go. Mr Mc an Bhaird (son of the bard), the Art teacher, was delighted to be with us. He would lead us around the Louvre and the Musée d'Orsay. Finally, hitting the ground running, we had Gemma Dawson. Miss Dawson moved at speed at all times. She taught PE. Our hearts sank. We could see her not bothering with the bus and making us walk everywhere.

There was still no sign of the baby. Cassie packed but worried about her mam. The woman could neither sleep nor rest at this stage. Her feet were swollen, and she was well overdue. If nothing happened, Cassie would have to stay at home. By the morning of Spy Wednesday, all three were in the hospital. The mam was coping, the dad was anxious, and poor Cassie was shaking with worry. The day dragged, but by teatime, a baby boy had arrived. He weighed eight and a half pounds, yawned and fell asleep.

When Cassie came out, she was smiling happily. She hugged me.

'They've picked his name already. He is gorgeous.'

'What are they calling him?'

'Christopher Joseph.'

'Wow. That's a good name.'

'He is named for both of his granddads.'

A new Christopher! I left her there with her family. I needed to be on my own. My feet took me to the cemetery. The headstone was granite, and etched upon it was his name, age and a quotation:

He is gone on the mountain,

He is lost to the forest,

Like a summer-dried fountain,

When our need was the sorest.

The font reappearing

From raindrops shall borrow,

But to us comes no cheering,

To Duncan no morrow.

I spoke it for him, told him how fine the block of granite was, and gave him the news about the baby. I suggested that he accompany me to Paris. He could fit in my pocket as he was now ethereal. He could have a rest day when we were in Euro Disney. I knew he would want to see the art at both museums.

'The baby's name is Christopher. Imagine. I will keep an eye on him as he grows. He will be as precious as you are.'

Cassie's mam was exhausted and would spend a few days in hospital. She told Cassie to get home and finish her packing. The dad walked around the ward whistling, carrying the new child close to his chest.

'When we return, I want you to come over to see him, Benny.'

I wanted that, too.

TWENTY FIVE

The hotel was beside the Gare du Nord. Part of a chain, all rooms were identical. We decided to spruce ourselves up to go out for dinner. We hit the showers, gelled our hair, changed shirts and were new men. The girls were new women, swanning around in short dresses and boots, holding tiny handbags stuffed to the brim.

Mr Mc an Bhaird let us know that he would have chosen a hotel elsewhere, maybe in the 5th arrondissement close to the Galeries Lafayette. Most students' parents couldn't have afforded that, though, so the Ibis would have to suffice.

Mr Mc was a Francophile and knew his way around. For dinner, he chose a local Italian. The family welcomed us. We began with a great antipasto of bread, olives and ham. Most of us ordered pizza. I looked forward to mine, and it didn't disappoint. The cheese, the crust, the ham were all a delight – it was almost a sensual experience. We had homemade ice cream to follow, with strong Italian coffee.

The evening was a great success. I wondered if Christopher had joined us. I could tell him all about it when I got home. I had no sense that he was nearby. In truth, my night was taken up with food, fun and friends.

Before we left, Miss Clancy sang 'The Rose of Tralee'. The grandpa sang 'Nessun Dorma'. Mr McCullough gave us 'O sole mio', and the daughter of the house silenced us with 'Un bel dì' from Madama Butterfly. Everyone clapped. Miss Clancy paid the bill. We rose as one to belt out 'The Fields of Athenry'. It would have been hard to beat for a first night in Paris.

We were kept busy each day with culture and the sights. Sitting on the steps of the Sacré-Cœur, the whole city laid out before us was magic. Drifting down the Seine in the dark, the lights shafting the water, the bridges ornate and old, was romantic and mellow. I had my girl by the hand, my arm around her to keep her warm, and her breath on my cheek. I was happy.

The Louvre was a mixed blessing. Howard, Ellen and Cassie were in a mathematical frame of mind. They discussed the glass pyramid geometrically, and figured out how to get the area of it, and the cubic capacity.

Seeing the 'Mona Lisa' was a must. We had to queue for ages, and I felt hot. I hardly noticed the other pictures. I just wanted to see it and go. I needed to get out of the fussing crowd. We were given thirty minutes to explore on our own.

So many of the paintings were very old, and I skipped right down to the Greek and Roman art on the lower ground floor. There was no one about, but I could feel the boy was with me.

The 'Venus de Milo' was magnificent.

'Benny, imagine seeing her with her arms as she was carved. Find the "Apollo of Mantua".'

I walked slowly, taking in the white marble figures, the plinths, the expressions on their faces, and their size. I took pictures with my phone, even a few selfies.

If he had anything else to say, he didn't share it. In the shop, I got postcards of the Venus, the Albino Lion and the Apollo. That was enough.

Mr Mc gave a talk that night. He made some suggestions about what to look for in the Musée d'Orsay. When he mentioned Van Gogh, I shivered. I knew that most of his famous works were in Amsterdam, but they also had some here in Paris!

'I'll say no more. Don't google anything. Go in and let your eyes be your guides.'

Cassie and Ellen agreed to explore together. Howard's main interest was that the building was originally a train station. I was happy to be going on my own because, with luck, I might be joined by a precious other. I did. I listened to 'Starry, Starry Night' in bed because Christopher was on my mind and in my heart.

I let myself be led through the different galleries and rooms. The colours everywhere were hot and pure. Though Van Gogh's works were my main focus, I realised that I should enjoy everything and allow the Impressionists time to engage me.

As I stood, humbled before Monet's 'The Artist's Garden at Giverny', I could feel a little whisper in my ear.

'Benny, this place is like good coffee. It must be savoured and tasted.'

I listened but felt no urge to respond.

'At last, the Van Gogh rooms,' he said.

I didn't want any conversation. I wanted to look and learn through my eyes.

'See there in "Self Portrait, 1887", the blues and yellows appear later in "Starry Night".'

'Starry Night Over the Rhône' held me silent for ages. There wasn't a word from him. I remembered the day he had found it online. It didn't have the magic of our 'Starry Night', which was many miles away in Amsterdam.

'The "Portrait of Dr. Gachet" should be of great interest to a historian like you.'

'Tell all,' I whispered.

'Well, there are two authenticated versions of this painting. One was acquired by the Städel Museum in Frankfurt in 1911. Göring, of Hitler fame, stole it and sold it. In May 1990, it sold at auction for $82.5 million. It cannot be located. This one here, the second version as owned by Dr Gachet himself, was bequeathed to France by his heirs.'

I was interested in those facts. Throughout World War Two, the Nazis had stolen art and artefacts from many countries, which were never returned. Art as spoils of war? It was ever thus.

There were ten of Vincent's works and we studied them all.

'I'll take my leave now,' he said, 'and let you get back to real people.'

'I have nothing to say, chap. We were supposed to go on art breaks for years. We had plans. It's all come back to me.'

Everyone was impressed by the Musée d'Orsay.

The talk on the bus was loud and exciting. People loved 'The Poppy Field'. The Impressionists were huge favourites. I knew I would return to complete the art breaks and see our plan through, however long it took.

We had day tickets for Euro Disney. We tried everything, but I drew the line at the Magic Kingdom. The girls saw everything there. We went on scary rides and did not go shopping. Cassie and Ellen shopped. It made no sense to me. You can buy Mickey Mouse and Minnie Mouse t-shirts in Penneys for a few bob. Why would you spend a small fortune to have a Disney label? I still had a lot to learn about girls.

They arrived wearing Minnie Mouse ears, sucking sticky soothers and wearing red, spotty bow ties. They took non-stop selfies. Meanwhile, Howard and I got burgers.

'I don't understand girls,' I said.

'Welcome to the club.'

'You understand Ellen.'

'God bless your innocence.'

'Well, ye've been going out for ages.'

'Ellen is a strong woman. She has plans in place for herself. I like order and planning. Our house is a shambles. Ellen gives me structure and meals with meat, for which I'm very grateful.'

'Do you love her?'

Silence.

'We never mention love, but I'm very attracted to her.'

'What if you break her heart?'

'I like Ellen, and I respect her. Anything can happen. We're having good fun. We respect each other. That's as much as I can give right now.'

'I love Cassie. I can't help myself.'

'In all honesty, Benny…'

'What?'

'You've had a crush on that girl since Sixth Class. I wonder if you know her at all.'

I was miffed and angry, and my face got red.

'Does she have a teddy bear?'

'I have no idea.'

'Which duvet cover does she like best?'

'How do you know her period is coming on?'

My eyes were like saucers. I knew nothing.

'I think you're confusing romance with love. You're still in the dewy-eyed stage. When you know her a bit better, see how you feel then.'

'I know her. I know that she loves art and books. She has had a hard time at home for ages. I have loved her since we were three.'

'A lot has changed since we were three. Be kind to her.'

The girls were waving at us and shouting. We had to run to the bus. They were all high on sugar. They ran and plonked themselves at the back of the bus. Miss Dawson warned them to keep the noise down. We all went for a rest, as this was our last night.

Mr Mc was determined that we experience the art of French cuisine, and decided on Chez Casimir for dinner. The owner was from Brittany, but weren't the Bretons of Celtic origin just like ourselves?

There was barely enough room for all of us. Other punters beat a hasty retreat as we advanced.

'Enough of you are studying French to be able to read the menus. You can have three courses on the set menu for thirty-five euros, or blow it all on a main course – drinks not included.'

I decided on a steak. I was famished and would demolish the meat, chips and salad with no problem. I found out how to say 'well done'. Soon, an element of disquiet set in. The people who picked from the set menu were tucking into their salad and vol au vents, while the rest of us salivated and gnashed our teeth.

My steak arrived swimming in gravy, with ten garden peas for company.

'Who knows,' I said to myself, 'this may be the French way.'

The frites arrived. Crisp and golden they were, but only warm. I cut the meat. Blood oozed out and blended with the gravy. The garden peas didn't seem to mind. I went to speak to Mr Mc.

'In France, they don't do "well done" as we do it at home. They consider ours to be a sin. You should have ordered chicken or veal.'

I returned to my seat to discover that Cassie had sorted it out. She explained to the waitress that I had misunderstood. Could they give the steak two more minutes on each side and heat the frites? No gravy, s'il vous plaît.

When my plate came back, I ate in total bliss. They gave me fresh frites, and the steak was Irish well done.

'You're an angel,' I mouthed over to her.

'Aren't you glad now that I did the six weeks away last summer?'

We got onto the red wine. Carafes of it just arrived, and we started drinking. There was no singing, but we had a great night.

We took our time strolling back, since we'd been

given an extra thirty minutes for curfew. We sat outside the hotel, enjoying the sky.

'You can't really see any stars, can you?'

'Light pollution.'

'Van Gogh managed to see the stars.'

From a seat far to the left of ours, one of the girls began to sing 'Starry, Starry Night', and it wasn't long before many voices joined in.

As those notes faded and I scanned the sky to find a star, I knew that my time with Christopher was coming to an end.

By the end of term, I had become familiar with Cassie's teddy bear, Jason, who resided on her work table. She liked the green duvet cover with pink flowers. This information made no difference to me, and it changed nothing. She had bad premenstrual cramps, but paracetamol and a warm hot water bottle helped. Just curling up beside her was lovely.

Something wasn't sitting right with me, though. I couldn't see the relevance of teddy bears or duvet covers. It was useful to know what girls and mothers had to suffer every month, but I wasn't her mother or her sister.

I saw Howard one day in The Dough Nut.

'You come in here on your own?'

'Why not?'

'I'd feel that everyone was looking at me.'

'Get a life, Benny. People are much too occupied with their own problems to be looking at you or me.'

'You're brave.'

'Me, never. The coffee is great, and I can read my book in peace and get a free top-up.'

'Is it a gothic novel?'

'Our gothic phase has come to a natural end. This is One Hundred Years of Solitude by Gabriel García Márquez.'

'Sounds heavy.'

'He's from South America. His genre is called magic realism.'

'I've never heard of it.'

'Each to their own, Benny.'

I ordered coffee for myself.

'Things aren't so good at home,' he said.

I had no idea what he was talking about.

'My parents are thinking of separating. My mam is away so much, she upsets everything when she returns. My dad is hopeless at running a house. For him, the only important thing is his work.'

'Have you talked to Ellen?'

'She's been a great support to me. My home was never a real family home like yours, but the idea of them splitting has hit me hard.'

I believed that nothing would be too much for Howard. With his brains and sense of curiosity, I thought he would always be able to find a solution – but I could also see that he might lay too much on Ellen's shoulders.

'Talk to Ellen again and listen to her. Listen to your own heart, Howard. You know where I am. Okay?'

Ellen got on his case. She told him to speak up for himself. He would have to get his parents to listen.

'Speak up for yourself. Your mam thinks she is real cool with her dreads and her leotard. She's stuck in the seventies.'

'Don't I know it. She listens to George Harrison's All Things Must Pass.'

'If she's determined to move to Amsterdam, she will unless you can shock her into reality. Remind her that she is abandoning you. Pull at her heartstrings, Howard. This is war.'

'In all fairness, Ellen, there are dudes in their seventies with dreads.'

'The leotards, Howard. Her belly sticks out!'

'Don't remind me.'

'A long, flowing skirt would be fine with the leotard. If she cut out the dreads and grew her own hair, she could look great.'

'I don't care how she looks. I want her to stay at home and act like my mother. And I want my dad to see that there's more to life than his job.'

TWENTY SIX

The final weeks in Transition Year were spent deciding on our subjects for Leaving Cert. We had the benefit of our work experience, our Junior Cert results and our aptitude tests. We had an idea of the areas we might choose.

I was invited up to meet the new Christopher. He had a head of black hair and smelled great. I held him carefully. He was very precious. I whispered to him, 'Hello, Christopher. That's a great name. I'll always look out for you.'

And I did. I kissed his forehead and then handed him to Cassie. She showed me sketches she had made of him, then took a picture of us on her phone.

I called down to see Andy and Eithne. They had come home for the summer, but would return to the States for the new semester. Eithne had abandoned the long plait, and her hair was now cut in a bob style, which suited her face.

I told them about Paris and that I had invited Christopher to come.

'He never comes to me now.'

'He doesn't come to us either.'

'There was a time when my need was huge. I would look out the window at night and search the sky for him.'

'We've talked about it. We think it's time to let him go. We can't keep calling him back. That time is gone.'

'Cassie's mam had a baby a few weeks ago. His name is Christopher. So, the name goes on.'

'Would you like to go up to his room, Benny?'

Nothing had been touched. His study table and chair, oak wardrobe and tattered teddy were there. Posters of Bowie, Einstein, Madonna and the LGBT rainbow flag. I looked through the bookshelf: The Catcher in the Rye, Nineteen Eighty-Four, Brave New World, Of Mice and Men and Brideshead Revisited.

I looked at his sketches and paintings. My boat at sea stared back at me from above his bed. Despite all his treasures, I found no sense of Christopher. His phantom self, who had come to my room and followed me to Paris, was more alive than any sense of him here.

'Take something from his room to remember him,' Eithne said.

'I won't take anything, Eithne. He gave me something when we were in Kerry, a token that means a lot to me. I'll always miss him. We wanted to grow up and be men together. We had planned art breaks all around Europe. End of story.'

His parents had that empty, grey look on their faces that would never fade. Grief carves itself into the hollows of faces and draws lines where previously there were none.

'I wonder what he would have put on his university

application. I think Theatre Studies.'

'You would be wide of the mark there, Benny. He wanted to do Pure English at Trinity. After that, he had planned to go to the University of East Anglia to do a master's in creative writing.'

'He wanted to be a writer?'

'He was already writing.'

They gave me a copy of his manuscript. I would read it by degrees. I hoped the words would resonate with me.

That is how I would keep Christopher alive.

A Boat for Benny

Mary Cotter

Printed in Great Britain
by Amazon